THE DOG JUDGE'S HANDBOOK

For Simon
(Ch. Sarae Chin Semillon)
. . . man could not have
asked for a better friend,
companion or confidant.

The Dog Judge's Handbook

by
Sari Brewster Tietjen

First Edition—First Printing
1980

HOWELL BOOK HOUSE INC.
230 Park Avenue
New York, N.Y. 10169

Library of Congress Cataloging in Publication Data

Tietjen, Sari Brewster.
   The dog judge's handbook.

   Bibliography: p. 223
   1. Dogs—Judging.   I. Title.
SF425.2.T43   636.7′0811   80-36820
ISBN 0-87605-512-9

e Muscle, 54 -
- External Ob-
bodorsal Fas-
cles, 59 - Rec-
oralis Muscle,
62 - Trapezius
, 64 - Tempor-
66 - Mandibu-
ideus Muscle,
69 - Cleidocer-
sarius Muscle,
leidobrachialis
e, 74 - Biceps
ii Muscle, 76 -
Carpi Radialis
ensor Muscle,
cle, 80 - Exten-
xtensor Carpi
cles, 83 - Obtu-
ndinosus Mus-

cle, 85 - Popliteal Lymph Gland, 86 - Anal Sphincter Muscle, 87 - Vaginal Sphincter Muscle, 88 -
Gracilis Muscle, 89 - Superficial Digital Flexor
Tendon, 90 - Bulbocavernosus Muscle and Bulb
of Penis, 91 - Testicle, 92 - Gastrocnemius Muscle.

D - THE FOURTH LAYER, THE BONES OR
SKELETON
93 - Digit (1st, 2nd, 3rd Phalanges), 94 - Metatar-
sal Bones, 95 - Tarsal Bones (Tarsus), 96 - Tibial
Tarsal Bone, 97 - Fibular Tarsal Bone, 98 - Tibia,
99 - Fibula, 100 - Sesamoid Bone, 101 - Patella,
102 - Femur, 103 - Ischium, 104 - Pubis, 105 -
Ilium, 106 - Os Penis, 107 - Coccygeal Vertebrae,
108 - Sacrum, 109 - Lumbar Vertebrae (7), 110 -
Thoracic Vertebrae (13), 111 - Ribs (13 pair),
112 - Cervical Vertebrae (7), 113 - Axis (2nd Cervical), 114 - Atlas (1st Cervical), 115 - Skull, 116 -
Canine Tooth, 117 - Mandible, 118 - Hyoid Ap-

paratus, 119 - Scapula, 120 - Sternum, 121 -
Costal Cartilages, 122 - Humerus, 123 - Radius,
124 - Ulna, 125 - Carpal Bones (Carpus), 126 -
Metacarpal Bones, 127 - 1st, 2nd and 3rd Phal-
angeal Bones (Digit).
THE ORGANS OF THE DOG

E - Right Side

F - Left Side
128 - Rectum, 129 - Male Urethra and Bulb of
Penis, 130 - Vagina, 131 - Testicles, 132 - Vas De-
ferens, 133 - Urinary Bladder, 134 - Ureter, 135 -
Kidney, 136 - Uterus, 137 - Ovary, 138 - Penis,
139 - Descending Colon, 140 - Small Intestine,
141 - Diaphragm, 142 - Caudal Lobe of Lung,
143 - Middle Lobe of Lung, 144 - Cranial Lobe of
Lung, 145 - Pericardium Surrounding Heart, 146 -
Spinal Cord, 147 - Brain, 148 - Trachea, 149 -
Esophagus, 150 - Liver, 151 - Stomach, 152 -
Spleen, 153 - Colon.

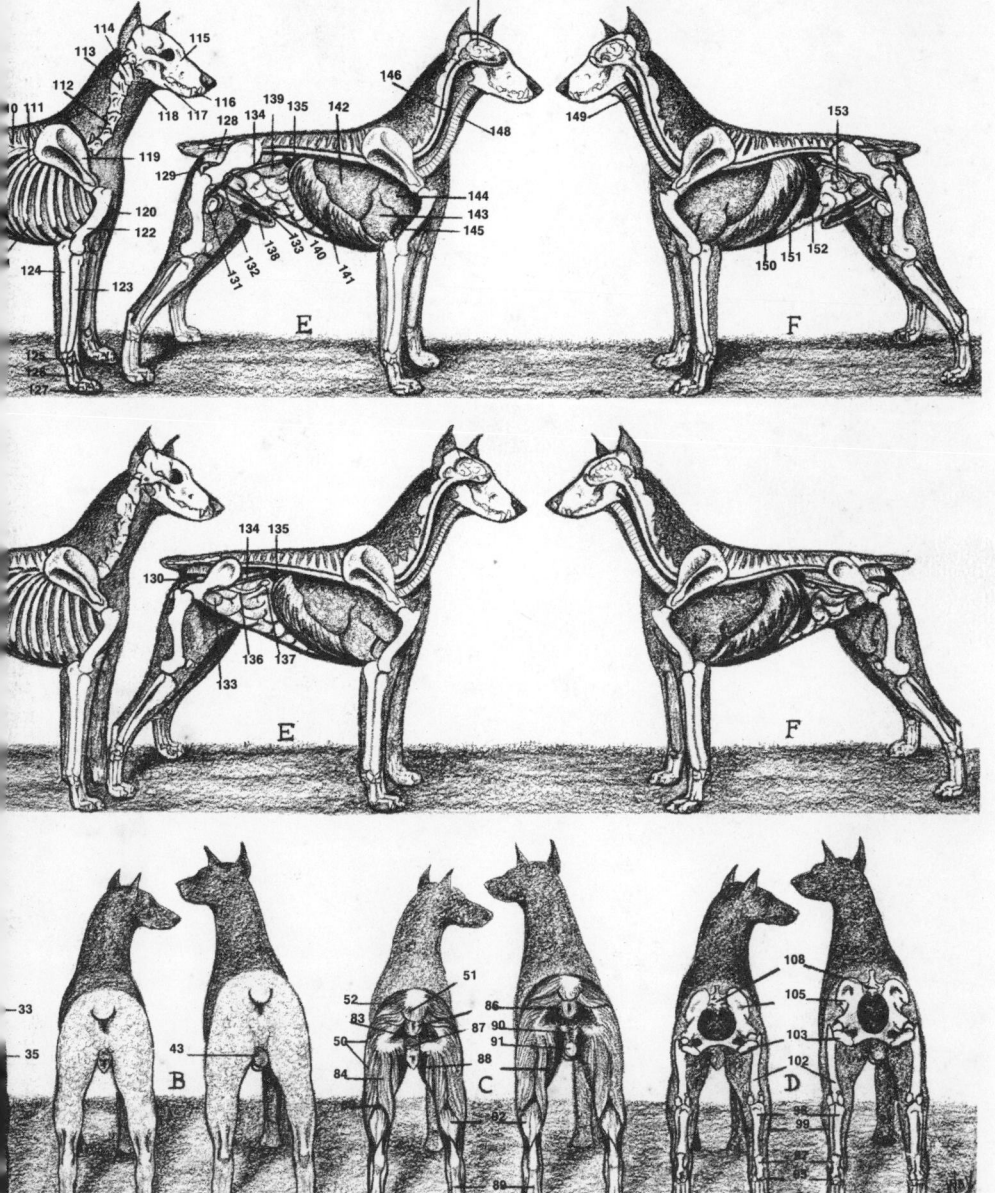

Contents

About the Author

SARI BREWSTER TIETJEN was born into the purebred dog fancy. Her mother, Mary S. Brewster, was an active and successful breeder and exhibitor with her Robwood Kennels of Toy breeds and others in the Hound, Working and Sporting groups. Mrs. Brewster has long been a highly respected judge of all Toys and several other breeds. Sari's sister, Joy Brewster, is an accomplished professional handler who received the "Fido" award for Dog Handler of the Year in 1979.

When she was only seven years old, Sari owned and showed her first champion. She won many firsts in Junior Showmanship but was unable to compete in the Westminster JS classes because they were always held at the same time she was showing her Japanese Spaniel (now named Japanese Chin) in the Toy Group.

During her show career, Sari trained, owned, bred and showed many dogs to championship and group wins. Her brace and team of Italian Greyhounds won groups and Best in Show when these competitions were more frequent than they are now. She financed purchase of her own foundation stock of Japanese Spaniels with winnings from shipboard horse races on the Queen Elizabeth during a trip to England. Until she gave up showing in favor of her judging career, she bred four generations of consistent group placing dogs. Now her son, Ricky, representing the third generation in this dog fancier family, has begun to show his own puppies.

At age 21 Sari started her judging career with AKC approval for Japanese Spaniels and Pomeranians. She is currently approved for all

Toy breeds, Lhasa Apsos, Bichon Frises, Keeshonden, Dalmatians and Poodles.

With a legal paraprofessional background, the author launched her writing career in public relations for political candidates and organizations. Her dog writings have included the Japanese Spaniel column for *The American Kennel Gazette,* dog columnist for the *Poughkeepsie Journal,* and numerous articles for *Showdogs, Shows & Dogs,* and the *Gazette* covering such topics as "Legally Providing for Your Dogs," "International Judging," "Victoria and Her Dogs," and "Dogs in Art."

Sari is also a popular lecturer and has appeared on radio and television interviews.

In this HANDBOOK she programs the education of a dog judge from the earliest preparatory steps—ringside observation, stewarding, match show judging, application to AKC—to consummate competence in ring procedure and decision making. She presents foolproof systems with detailed examples for handling assignments.

She tells how to avoid judging pitfalls, how to cope with protests, gifts and poison pen letters. She includes sample bookkeeping records and Federal Income Tax forms for judging expenses and income. An especially valuable chapter gives the answers to 91 questions concerning procedural problems a judge may encounter. The AKC connection is explicitly covered with quotations from AKC officials.

The highly useful information in this HANDBOOK reflects the author's deep experience in the dog sport and her meticulous research among other judges, dog show officials and superintendents, and key AKC executives.

The publishers are pleased to present this worthy work so that aspiring and experienced dog show arbiters will, to quote the author herself, "thoroughly enjoy judging for the challenge it presents!"

Preface

THE IDEA FOR THIS BOOK was conceived while watching a judge flounder in making a simple procedural decision while in the ring. As this was an approved group judge, it quickly came to mind that there are few sources available for a person to turn to when in doubt. No books, magazine articles or other written materials quite cover the subject of judging dogs in enough detail to offer the guidance that is needed. And to compound the problem, an approved judge cannot very well turn to the American Kennel Club for answers to basic questions. After all, when one becomes a judge the assumption is that he has the knowledge to meet any and all problems. Unfortunately this is a misconception. Judging is a constant learning experience and each new show presents its own set of enigmas that must be resolved. Not only is it difficult for new judges to acquire the background, knowledge and experience to adjudicate comfortably in the ring, but established judges may also need a refresher from time to time.

This Handbook was envisioned to be a source that covers in depth all aspects of judging from an explanation of procedures required in applying for new and additional breeds, initial show contacts, record keeping and correspondence, to preparation for the show itself. There is a comprehensive section on the mental and physical aspects of judging, as well as the procedural methods. The section on how to use a wicket was developed because judges need clear, concise instructions on its application before venturing to use it in the ring. Traveling is covered in detail as many judges spend more time on the road than at the show grounds.

Although directed to all potential, new and experienced judges. a secondary underlining fact is the value of the text to the dog fancy at large. It is hoped that by presenting an insight into what it is like to become and be a judge, breeders, exhibitors and handlers will understand their judges and apply this understanding before labeling them on the basis of whether one wins or loses. Categorize your judges, if you will, but do so on their actual merit.

As you read this text, you will note that the judge is always identified by the pronoun "he." This was merely done for ease of reading and in no way reflects a superior stance upon male counterparts.

Sari B. Tietjen
Rhinebeck, New York

Acknowledgments

MUCH OF WHAT YOU READ herein is based upon a consensus that was derived from correspondence, phone calls and personal interviews with hundreds of judges and dog fanciers throughout the country. It would be impossible to thank each and every one of them in print, but as they know who they are I hope the value of the work presented is an acknowledgment of their time and consideration.

Of the judges whom I personally interviewed there were seven in particular who gave multiple hours and deep consideration to my project: Anne Rogers Clark, Kitty Drury, Bill Kendrick, Chet Collier, Henry Stoecker, Peter Thomson and Jim Trullinger.

I spent some time in Greensboro, North Carolina viewing the Moss-Bow/Foley operation first hand and quizzing their superintendents on experiences, suggestions and ideas. This insight into another aspect of the dog scene was invaluable in offering the total picture.

Many breed clubs responded to my query on judicial seminars and breed booklets. The excerpts of some of the illustrations contained in *The Standard Schnauzer Illustrated* are but a few of the many fine features contained in this booklet prepared by Mary Cole Schofield and illustrated by Gail B. MacKiernan for the Standard Schnauzer Club of America.

My gratitude to Robert F. Way, VMD, MS for permission to include in this book his Doberman Pinscher anatomical illustrations.

My appreciation to the American Kennel Club for permission to reprint illustrations that had first appeared in *Pure-Bred Dogs—*

American Kennel Gazette during the 1920's and 30's.

The fantastic step-by-step pictures on how to use a wicket are the result of superb photography by John Ashbey and the patience of his wife Janet's Dalmatian.

Jayne Langdon and Edd Bivin met in California to put together the photos which accompany the suggestions for the most advantageous way to pose for pictures.

It goes without saying that many pages of this book would not be worth the paper the words are printed on without the assistance of the American Kennel Club. The open doors I found wherever I turned (and I turned through many) are deeply appreciated. Much of the success of this enterprise lies in the willingness of many to answer a constant barrage of questions. Besides my family, I am sure that no other persons were more relieved when the last page was finished. I am especially indebted to Bill Stifel, Chuck O'Neill, Len Brumby, Bill Schmick, Norm Furber, Frank Harra and Monroe Stebbins for their help.

In acknowledging the many persons who played a vital role in the creation of this manuscript, I must express special thanks to those close to me who gave so freely of their support, guidance and understanding; my mother, Mary S. Brewster, without whose interest in dogs I could not have written this book; my sister, Joy, who as a handler gave me a different point of view and was always presenting questions; my brother, Jack, who I saddled with the on-going responsibility of finding parts for a typewriter that kept insisting on breaking down; Joan who, as my typist, learned a lot about dogs in the process; Chet who read the initial draft and kept advising me to cut lest I put everyone to sleep by the end of the first chapter; Herman whose level head, constant support and advice was always present; Ricky who finally understood that his mother is certainly more creative with a typewriter than she will ever be with a sewing machine; and last, but definitely not least, my Japanese Chins who often kept me company and offered necessary diversions.

1

Becoming a Judge
Helpful Hints

WANTED: Person willing to stand on his/her feet for up to nine hours at a stretch with a five- to ten-minute interval for lunch and one-minute recess for laps to the john; compelled to endure heatstrokes and frostbites and not flinch during thunderstorms, hurricanes or snow showers; must be sprightly and vivacious even though the toes are going to disown the feet and the body repudiates the head as it endures over 175 deep knee bends; needs to be willing to subject oneself to verbal abuse, be on guard for crafty tricks and alerted to the management's eagle eye: should be able to differentiate between a four-footed canine and a two-footed human and blank one's mind out as to previous encounters; necessary to attend various social functions, digest shoe leather often misdiagnosed as prime ribs and stay at hostels that feature lumpy beds, cold showers and crickets for company. Pay—impecunious. Self-esteem—immeasurable. This job is only for those who are thick of skin, quick of mind and fast on feet. Apply to the American Kennel Club, 51 Madison Avenue, New York, New York 10010.

Do you know what position the job description refers to? Do you want to apply? Have you the necessary qualifications? Are you willing to endure the hardships described above? Do you know what you are letting yourself in for?

If you answered yes to all five questions, read on. If your answer was no to any of them, you may lack the necessary dedication, but read on anyway. You might be able to use the knowledge gathered from this text to your benefit either in the show ring or at cocktail parties where tidbits on the dog scene are more tantalizing than Washington's latest scandals.

The job description is obviously for that of an approved American Kennel Club judge of pure-bred dogs. Those who indicated their interest in holding such a formidable title may wonder if they have taken leave of their senses. They might very well ask, who in their right mind would be willing to subject themselves to such an arduous task? Perhaps the answer lies in the basic human desire to accept challenges and conquer new frontiers. In judging dogs, every show is different. Just as the dogs vary, so too do the problems and circumstances that surround each decision. The human mind needs to rise to the occasion and the body must endure while the sole arbiter in the ring is looked at with both reverence and disdain by handlers, breeders and exhibitors alike. The self-esteem derived from performing the task justly, honestly and satisfactorily cannot be measured on any chart or scale. On the other hand, the insecure adjudicator will have his ego downtrodden to the pits by those who are aware of his lack of knowledge. Nevertheless, "the mountain highs will outweigh the valley lows" as the dedicated judge ventures onward and upward.

To reach such a status, a judge has to spend long hours studying his breed/breeds: attend many shows to observe judging and talk to exhibitors; become well-versed in the rules and regulations and proper ring procedure; and meet the requirements of the AKC in passing interviews, examinations and the provisional period. Even then, after obtaining approval, the learning process does not stop. It never stops as conscientious persons are always watching and listening for new insights into their avocation. If you are willing to meet this challenge, let's continue as we lay the path to judging dogs.

Background

It is difficult to fully define the background required to become an adjudicator of dogs. Unlike other professions, like law or medicine, where one has to have a college diploma, specialty degree and pass state exams, the judging field does not have such definitive requirements. Rather, it is generally accepted that a person must have a viable working knowledge of the dog game. This includes having participated in a successful breeding program and having been an accomplished exhibitor.

To have his application for approval to judge dogs seriously considered, a potential judge must prove his active involvement in the dog world. The AKC cares not for a specified time frame, such as five or ten years of showing dogs. They look instead at the depth of interest, the broad spectrum of knowledge and the possession of judicial bearing that every successful judge must maintain.

It is not enough for you, the potential judge, to attend a few shows a year. If you are resolute, you will find yourself relinquishing most of your spare time to learning about the position you wish to obtain. This means attending every conceivable show in your area, purchasing and reading books and periodicals, becoming active in dog related organizations, stewarding, participating in match show judging and attending seminars. In short, every opportunity that comes your way, which will further enhance your education, needs to be fully explored.

The Ideal Judge

Before you can proceed any further in your quest to learn about judging, you should form an image in your mind of what makes an ideal judge and mold yourself to fit that conception.

A hypothetical prototype stands tall, not in physical size, but in presence. He is self-confident without being egotistical, poised without being stuffy and relaxed without being nonchalant. He takes his job seriously and yet knows that the weight of the world does not rest on his shoulders. He is friendly, patient and understanding with both the four-footed canines and their sometimes stumbling masters.

He controls his ring; the ring does not control him. Before he judges he surveys the scene, decides the best way to use the area and proceeds in a regulated, disciplined manner. Nevertheless if circumstances warrant, he is flexible enough to change.

The judge is attired in an outfit that is both fitting of the task assigned to him and the climatic conditions he may confront that day. The clothes have an aura of authority and power that makes a judge a person to be looked up to and respected. They must be well-cut, fitted properly and of good material. Understated, clothing will not outshine the person but rather be a part of the overall picture.

And finally this judge has fully prepared himself, both physically and mentally, to meet the challenges that lie before him. He knows the breeds he is to adjudicate, has studied the standards and conversed with owners, breeders and handlers about particular problems facing the breed(s) at that time. He is fully aware of proper ring procedures and applies the official rules in a justifiable fashion. Aware of the ramifications of his decisions, he does not make lightly nor in jest. He will not favor friends, play games, fall for carefully designed traps or take the easy way out.

A judge is not God—he does have days when nothing seems to go right, when he will make unthinking errors and idiotic mistakes. An occasional lapse is permitted and understood, for after all, he is human and one of us. Therefore, we will not penalize him for his human frailties as together we all strive for the betterment of the dog world.

Personality and Temperament

Anyone who thinks that the person who stands front and center in the middle of the dog show ring, upon whose shoulders the decisions rest for that day, has an easy time of it is sadly mistaken. For judicial deductions are only arrived at after a great deal of time, thought and energy on the part of the arbitrator.

Not everybody possesses the wherewithal to perform in the ring. It is not uncommon for the greatest breeders, who outside of the ring can pick the best dogs right and left, to freeze up when they have to make the very same decisions on the inside. And there are those persons who lack the backbone to make evaluations solely based on the dogs as they are that day in the ring—not on previous records, other wins under the same judge or being owned or handled by tried and true friends or bitter enemies.

Judicial temperament becomes as important as judicial bearing. It is not enough to look the part of a judge and function with judicial demeanor. You must also walk a fine line between being too stern and overly zealous in the personality you radiate while in the ring. You must appear to be taking your task seriously, yet have the ability to yield or bend as situations arise. A pleasing smile, willing handshake and freely given advice join equally with the capability of making decisions, being objective and courageous. A good judge has the qualities to evenly balance all these factors.

Another element necessary to functional judging is the ability to

16

completely black out everything else that is happening around the show grounds. One of a judge's principal requirements must be to wear imaginary blinders that restrict his field of vision to his ring and its occupants. No thought should be given to outside distractions. Friends are not there to be chatted with about the latest gossip, nor are dogs walking outside the ring to be observed. Even a scantily clad female or male wearing tight pants must be ignored as the judge concentrates solely on his ring.

It is necessary to be resolute in not only ignoring obvious diversions, but also in forgetting that others are watching not just the dogs and their handlers, but also the judge. It is easy to be so self-conscious about your appearance that you lose sight of the total picture. There is a misconception that a judge, and only the judge, is the center of attention and every detail of that person's being is carefully and sometimes diabolically scrutinized. The judge is but a part of the whole and once this is understood it can be acknowledged as such.

Another danger to reckon with is the basic human desire to please. No one wants to hurt another and everyone wants to be well thought of by all. As a judge this is an impossible goal to achieve. Practically speaking there are many more losers than winners, which affords plenty of opportunity for disagreements to arise. The arbiter who tries to please everyone ends up pleasing no one, including himself.

The picture painted is not a bleak one, but practical and honest. If you are still interested in applying for the job, let's continue and probe into your future.

Observing at Shows

The first inkling you may have had about exploring the concept of judging was not a strange tingling sensation in your toes, nor a quickened palpation of the heart. Instead this alien desire may have seemed to have come out of the blue with no flourish of trumpets sounding in the distance.

What probably happened is that in watching judging at shows, either as an exhibitor or a spectator, you discovered a keen interest in that end of the sport. Perhaps, you observed some inept adjudicator and felt that you could have performed better in the same circumstances, or you watched someone you really admire and decided that by emulating that person you in turn could become a better human being. For whatever the reason, you feel you are now ready to seriously consider the path to judging.

Attending shows strictly as an observer is the first step for any would-be judge. Fido should stay home, where he no doubt would prefer to be anyway, and the kids could be better served by being permitted to romp around their neighborhood instead of the show grounds. Unless the spouse is doggy and independent, a clinging vine is not needed or helpful. Nor are drinking buddies desired companions. The idea is not to partake in a social occasion, but to involve oneself in an educational experience.

Select a show where a judge whom you particularly admire is officiating. Observing an ignominious arbitrator will either lead you astray or turn you off completely from the whole concept. Study the standards the night before the show for those breeds which you are particularly interested in watching and plan on arriving at the show grounds in plenty of time.

, Once at the show do whatever socializing you feel you must do well ahead of judging time. It is not necessary to announce to one and all your yearnings for judgehood, nor command friends to sit beside the ring while you loudly proclaim that you know more than anyone else. Even observing must be approached in a business-like fashion and you need to conduct yourself appropriately.

The conscientious person will find a good position outside the ring to watch the dogs while they are stacked and examined and to observe their movement. Generally this is near where the judge is individually examining the dogs and in direct line with the gaiting pattern. Standing is very often better than sitting as you can usually see better and are able to move about as you find the positions changing. You need to be able to watch exactly what the judge is doing with his hands, trace his findings in your mind and try to draw your own conclusions, albeit allowing for a margin of error. Observe the movement and see if it coincides with your thoughts on the structure. As each dog is scrutinized, place it in the class in your mind, or use the catalog marking on the right side opposite the dog's name, your placement and reasons.

When the judge has made his decision, mark his findings on the left side in the catalog. If you vehemently disagree with his conclusions, state why. This procedure makes you think and ask questions of yourself—what did the judge see that I did not? Does the animal have a fault I could not detect? Have I overlooked or misinterpreted the standard?

If the judge is a personal friend, go up to him after he has completed his entire assignment for the day and ask any questions you may have. Most judges are willing to assist in any way that they can, but you should remember that if the assignment was long the judge may not be able to recall particular dogs. This is where your notes may be helpful. When talking with him, do not challenge his decisions or offer opinions of your own. Let him know that you are learning and are interested in whatever comments he may have about that breed. If you are unable to resolve a specific point in your mind, store it for further inquiry of a few breeders.

By observing judging in this manner, you have been able to parenthetically place yourself in the ring in a position of having to make selections based on a methodical, concise evaluation.

As you go along, and observing is not a one time experience, you will expand your interests into other breeds either within the same group or not. You will discover that you want to stay at the show from its beginning to its conclusion, as you become engrossed in watching, learning and listening. You will be building up a repertoire of facts and encounters to draw upon in the future.

It is important to note that no matter where your interests lie, you can forever learn, expand your knowledge and improve upon yourself, if you are willing to partake in every opportunity available to you.

Stewarding

How many times have we all sat back and wondered about the benefits of stewarding? It goes without saying that a competent steward makes all the difference in the world as to whether or not the judge has a good day, stays on time and is able to be calm and cool regardless of any crisis.

A potential adjudicator would be well advised to avail himself of the opportunity to volunteer for a couple of stints of stewardship. This is the only occasion where he has the chance to be in the ring, experiencing some of what a judge must endure, without having a four-footed canine tugging at the other end of the lead.

In the ring, the steward's first priority is to assist the judge in whatever way he can. Usually the judge advises him of the ring procedure that he will use, how absentees are to be handled, where to place ribbons and/or trophies and so on. But from the would-be judge's point of view, the opportunity to view the judge's book and observe procedure and how records are kept should not be overlooked as one of the most vital aspects of his education.

Stewarding, therefore, enables the prospective arbitrator to pick up some first hand observations of what goes on in the ring and a glimpse of some of the thought processes judging requires.

Match Show Judging

American Kennel Club sanctioned match shows, fun matches, futurities and sweepstakes afford excellent opportunities for clubs, judges, exhibitors and dogs to participate in total learning experiences.

As "trial runs" match shows have many advantages: newly formed clubs use their first informal shows as a means of demonstrating that they have the capability to function as a show giving club; older clubs continue the tradition as a proving ground for new members; some clubs try out new ideas at matches before converting them for point shows; A match also provides a method of raising funds and advocating pure-bred dogs to the general public.

For exhibitors and their dogs, these shows offer the least expensive way for them to see if they are or are not suitable for point shows. They can learn first hand the ecstasy of winning and the agony of defeat. Those, who tend to be all thumbs and wind themselves and their charges into knots as they constantly step on each other's toes (and the judge's as well), will find that the informal shows can help them in overcoming their fears as they gradually become more familiar with the process.

Dogs that have been sheltered will quickly either adapt to the hustle and bustle or give up completely. Puppies are afforded the first chance to show their stuff.

But what about the judges? Must persons who are desirous of attaining AKC recognition participate in these informal shows? Once approved, do they have to continue?

To all of the above, yes. Anyone who would like to expand his dog show activity into the world of judging would be well advised to acquaint himself with the opportunities presented at matches, sweepstakes and futurities. For this is the only time he can step into the ring as an arbitrator and evaluate the dogs on hand in circumstances comparable to point shows. One will be able to see if he possesses those characteristics needed to be a judge and if he really wants to be in the position of having to make the kind of decisions that judging entails. It is necessary to learn the task at hand, to absolve oneself from having been on the other side of the lead and to concentrate solely on the animals to be evaluated.

At match shows, there is not necessarily a strict time element to contend with and the judge gets plenty of practice in dealing with fumbling exhibitors and Fidos that will not walk. As patience is the theme for the day, our judge can take the time carefully and completely to weigh the dogs against his intrepretation of the standard, which he studied the night before, and against each other. He can practice developing his "eye," ring procedure and gaining confidence in making decisions.

Since one is usually asked to officiate over an entire group or more, the judge has the chance to use all he has learned by studying the breeds for which he is mainly interested in applying for AKC approval, as well as others of the same group. He will be able to understand the interaction of some family breeds and will clearly comprehend that not all breeds are alike and require judging in the same manner. By expanding his realm of interest, he will become more cognizant of dogs as a whole rather than just a part.

Informal shows are not only good for the prospective participant, but also for the approved judge who wishes to expand his breeds. Judges should try to officiate over those breeds they are not approved to do at point shows. By restricting the match show judging to new breeds, they are giving themselves the opportunity to further their education on those breeds in which they would like to expand their knowledge for eventual approval.

For all the benefits of judging match shows, there are some deterrents which should be acknowledged and taken in stride. Generally the quality leaves much to be desired and some persons will have difficulty in choosing the best from the worst. Also, some clubs run their matches in such a lackadaisical fashion that the inexperienced judge may have a dilemma in trying to determine which end is up. One needs to be cautioned not to let personal dissatisfaction or confusion with one show become so disheartening that he is quickly discouraged and abandons all hope of seeking full approval.

Attending Seminars

Many clubs sponsor educational seminars. The rap sessions may encompass a specific breed or breeds, if put together by a breed club or combination of a few clubs, or may cover a realm of topics all concerned with dogs and their structure. Unfortunately, as of this writing, very few clubs cover judging techniques, ring procedures or universal how-to.

If a seminar is being held in your area, even if not covering the breeds you may be specifically interested in, attend if possible. You never know what little tidbit or two you pick up might be applicable to all breeds and could help you in understanding more about dogs in general.

It has to be said that seminars are only as good as the people who present them and this thought should always be kept in the back of your mind. Personal self-serving discussions do little to enhance anyone's future. Breed talks that refuse to present adequately and honestly the pluses and minuses of the dogs on hand are shirking their responsibilities.

Ask questions, disagree if you wish, but do not argue. Attend with an open mind, but study the breed standard beforehand. By realizing that this is to be an educational experience and not a social one, you will leave a little wiser and know that your time and money was not ill spent. However, there is one proviso—the seminar must live up to its billing and emphasize quality rather than quantity.

Reading Material

Any potential judge would be well advised to read as much source material as possible. Although one may not find the subject matter as titillating as one of the more popular novels of the day, there is much to be learned from thoroughly researched, well-written articles and books.

The American Kennel Club has several booklets available for the prospective judge. You should write and procure copies of the *Rules Applying to Registration and Dog Shows* and the *Judge's Guidelines*.

The Complete Dog Book, also sponsored by the AKC, is another must. Other general dog books, including those covering structure and gaiting, should be considered as well as some of the better breed books covering the specific breeds you are interested in pursuing. Judging books, likewise, offer an effective medium for studying about the task you wish to undertake. Further recommendations cover some foreign books and oldtimers as a way of broadening your scope and deriving a variety of opinions.

Contacting breed clubs should not be forgotten as a few of the clubs publish excellent material on their breeds and suggestions as to the correct way to judge the specific breeds.

All-breed, group and breed magazines use advertising of wins as a means of sustaining the periodicals. However, sandwiched in between the photographs can be found some superb articles, as opposed to those which are construed as gossipy in intent, which should be read and re-read.

One note on pictures: it is interesting to observe that while pictures advertising wins hype the dogs involved, a studious perusal of all aspects of the pictured animal will help in assisting the forthcoming judge to learn different breed types and prevalent faults.

See the "Resource Section" in the back for some suggested reading material.

Record Keeping

The most frequently overlooked aspect required of not only every potential judge, but approved judge as well, is that of record keeping. Maintaining proper records entails not only the obvious areas such as calendars and expenses (more on these in subsequent chapters) but also careful records should be kept covering detailed dog educational background.

A sectionalized notebook suffices in establishing separate portions devoted to showing, breeding and organizational participation. Other sections should include reading matter, seminar material and your findings in attending shows as an observer, talking with breeders, stewarding and match show assignments.

Your records should cover your impressions of what you saw, experienced and anything you learned. For an example, if in observing judging you witnessed a particular technique that you really liked, make note of it. Or if you saw something you wish to avoid, write it down. The same applies to dogs shown. If there was one which attracted you the most, its name, breeder and owner, or a torn sheet from the catalog listing devoted to the particular dog should appear in your book. Beneath this information list what you liked most of all about the dog and where you considered his faults to lie. If unsure about a specific point or if you feel you needed to be able to place your hands on the animal, make reference to these facts as well. If after the judging you were able to talk with the exhibitor and examine the dog, report your findings.

If there is a special article in a magazine which seems to hit a subject just right, tear it out and place it in your notebook for a reference guide.

Keep any information handed out at seminars, as well as notes you may have made.

After judging futurities, sweepstakes or match shows make note of the breed or breeds, entry and quality of the dogs shown. If the show was disorganized or failed to follow accepted patterns, jot this down as well.

As you can see, your notebook will soon be overflowing as you devote more time and energy to achieving your ultimate goal, and you may need to expand to another one.

The notebook idea, which needs constant updating during your judging career, is a valuable tool that serves two purposes:

1) If you take it with you when you are personally interviewed by the AKC on your application approval, it will be an at-hand reference guide for your use, may back up a particular statement and will be evidence of your involvement and devotion.

2) What you learned can never be permanently forgotten when you establish a system that places all vital educational material readily available for a quick glance and if you use it to refresh your memory. You will find, as time goes on, that you will be continuously referring to your guide and be comforted by the fact that such information is easily at hand.

To become a judge, one has to spend long hours studying.
Foster—GAZETTE, American Kennel Club

24

2

Who Can Be a Judge

B EFORE YOU PURSUE this question of judging any further, you had best be sure you are over 21 years of age and meet the standard requirements for judges as listed in Chapter 10, Section 1 of the AKC's Rules and Regulations:

"Any reputable person who is in good standing with the American Kennel Club may apply for leave to judge any breed or breeds of pure-bred dogs which in his or her opinion he or she is qualified by training and experience to pass upon, with the exception of persons connected with any publication in the capacity of solicitor for kennel advertisements, persons connected with dog food, dog remedy or kennel supply companies in the capacity of solicitor or salesman, persons employed in and about kennels, persons who buy, sell and in any way trade or traffic in dogs as a means of livelihood in whole or in part, whether or not they be known as dealers and professional show superintendents.

"No judge shall be granted a license to be an annual superintendent. No judge shall be eligible to judge any assignment at a licensed or member show if he or she resides in the same household with any person who does not meet the occupational eligibility requirements to judge as described in this section."

Applying for Initial Breeds

By this time you should have made a definite decision on the exact breed or breeds you would like to be able to judge at point shows. Do not apply for an assortment of breeds and be willing to take your chances on what you will get. It is not improbable that you could receive approval for the very breed that you know the least about and would do a poor job of judging. Likewise, you certainly would not want to flunk your provisional because you are not really confident of the breed granted. Therefore, apply for only the breed or breeds for which you can substantiate background, knowledge and understanding.

Write to the American Kennel Club, in care of the Judges' Department, for the necessary application forms. You will receive within a week or two the following packet containing the application, questionnaire, written exam and informational data concerning the steps required for consideration of provisional status—see following pages.

After swiftly glancing at all the documents, set everything aside until you have a chance to study the material in peace and quiet. Do not succumb to an initial reaction of horror at the seemingly endless and impossible questions. Only after taking the opportunity to carefully scrutinize all the papers will you see that a continuity does exist and, although you may consider the steps to be difficult, they will not be impossible if you did your homework as outlined in Chapter 1. Much of the general information requested centers on many of the details you were working so arduously on—exhibiting, breeding, match show and stewarding experiences, and the like. It becomes quite clear that the application is merely a form to assist the AKC in trying to determine whether you possess the necessary qualifications to become a judge.

With pencil and eraser in hand, begin making drafts of your answers on scrap sheets of paper. By doing this you can correlate all the information and gather your thoughts without ruining the original forms. Nothing could impede your progress quicker than submitting papers covered with scratchouts and crossovers requiring an unknown code to decipher.

Listed below are the primary prerequisites taken into consideration by the Board of Directors when reviewing Provisional Breed Applications. Although meeting the minimum requirements will not guarantee that Provisional Judging Status will be granted, neither will the failure to meet the requirements in one (1) area (I — V only) preclude approval as it is an applicant's total background and experience that is taken into consideration.

In general, the Board bases their decision upon the following criteria:

I.   Have owned several dogs of the Breed Applied For.

II.   Evidence breeding experience in the Breed Applied For. (For the average applicant, this translates into 5 or 6 litters.)

III. Have stewarded at a minimum of 5 AKC Member or Licensed Shows.

IV.   Have judged a minimum of 6 Sanctioned Matches, Sweepstakes or Futurities.

V.   Have a strong overall background and involvement in the sport of dogs, such as Club memberships or other affiliations relating to the sport.

VI.   Must have compiled a record of exhibiting at Dog Shows over a minimum of 8 years.

VII. Applicants must pass a comprehensive written examination which requires a thorough understanding of AKC rules and policies.

VIII. A Personal Interview will be required. Upon receipt of your application, it is processed and screened. After this is completed, a personal interview will be arranged. This is a service designed to assist applicants to get a clear understanding of AKC rules and policies toward judging, and to provide AKC with the opportunity to become acquainted with persons aspiring toward approval to judge.

IX.   All applicants must meet the Occupational eligibility requirement under AKC Rules as stated in the "Dog Show Rules," Chapter 10, Section 1. Favorable action will not be taken if this requirement cannot be met regardless of an individual's show and breeding experience.

After the initial screening, the applicants' names together with the breeds for which they are applying will be published in the first available issue of the Gazette in order that interested persons can offer their opinions of the applicants' qualifications.

Two (2) months following publication in the Gazette, all applications will be submitted to a Staff Committee and then to a Board Committee for their review and recommendations.

Three (3) months following publication in the Gazette, all applications will be submitted to the Board of Directors for consideration for Provisional Judging Status. If approved by the Board of Directors, the applicants' names together with the breeds for which approval is granted will be published in the Gazette as Provisional Judges.

Once your application has been considered by the Board of Directors, you will be promptly notified of the action taken. Please do not call AKC as this information will not be given out over the phone.

Should you be granted Provisional judging status, you must complete a minimum of three (3) judging assignments in each of the breeds approved before requesting consideration for regular judging status. However, a Provisional judge may accept an unlimited number of assignments in the breeds for which they are approved to judge.

In order for the Board of Directors to consider a Provisional judge for Regular Judging Status, the Provisional Judge must make this request to AKC in writing indicating the three (3) assignments judged and the total entry judged for each assignment. Upon receipt of this notification, the Provisional's record will be submitted to the Board of Directors at its earliest meeting possible.

THE AMERICAN KENNEL CLUB
JUDGES DEPARTMENT

Informational letter which accompanies the potential provisional judge's packet.

AMERICAN KENNEL CLUB - 51 Madison Avenue, New York, NY 10010

JUDGING APPLICATION

* If your answer to question #7 is "Yes", please submit a letter with your application giving your assurance that if you are approved to judge you will completely divorce yourself from the practice of handling dogs and any related practices such as boarding, grooming and conditioning dogs.

1. Name (Print) _____ Home Phone _____
    Area Code   No.

    Home Address _____
    No.   Street   Town City   State   Zip

2. Date of Birth _____ Place of Birth _____

3. I am applying for approval to Judge the following Breed(s) _____

    _____

4. Since what year have you *continuously* owned one or more dogs of the breed(s) you are applying for (specify year for each breed, i. e., Pointers - 1960):

    _____

    _____

    On the attached BLUE SHEET give registered names and breeds of several of them.

5. At how many shows did you exhibit on a yearly average _____
    Average Per Year

    On the attached YELLOW SHEET list the shows, by year, in which you have exhibited dogs.

6. Have you ever held a Handlers License _____ If Yes, from _____ to _____
    Yes/No   Year   Year

7. Are you or have you ever been a Professional Handler. The term "Professional Handler" applies to all persons who represent themselves through a rate card or otherwise as handling dogs in the show ring for pay. _____ If Yes, from _____ to _____.
    Yes No   Year   Year

8. Do you reside in the same household with a Professional Handler? _____ If Yes, state handler's name

    _____

9. Do you have any active memberships in dog clubs _____ If Yes, on the attached PINK SHEET, list clubs and any office held.
    Yes No

    Are you a delegate _____ If Yes, indicate club _____
    Yes No

10. Are you a full time resident of the U.S. _____ If No, please explain. _____
    Yes No

11. Do you have any physical handicaps _____ If Yes, describe them _____
    Yes No

    _____

12. Business, Profession or Occupation (Specify Title and Job Description) _____

    _____

13. Firm Name (or "self-employed") _____

    Business Address _____ Phone _____
                        No.   Street   *Area Code   No.*

    _____
                Town-City   *State*   *Zip*

14. Are you or have you ever been employed in and about kennels _____ If Yes, give details on attached PINK
    SHEET.   *Yes No*

15. Do you maintain a boarding kennel _____ If Yes, indicate location, how long you have been operating it, and if
                                       Yes No

    the dogs boarded are show specimens or pets _____

    _____

    _____

16. Do you or any member of your immediate family or household prepare, condition or handle dogs for others
    _____ Are you compensated *in any way* _____
    Yes No   *Yes No*

    If Yes to either or both, give explanation on attached PINK SHEET.

17. Do you have dog(s) at Stud _____ If Yes, on attached PINK SHEET indicate their name(s) and breed(s).
                               Yes No

18. Do you buy dogs for resale _____ If Yes, please explain in detail. _____
                               Yes No

    _____

    _____

    _____

    Do you buy dogs to improve your breeding stock _____
                                                    Yes No

    In instances where you sell dogs, do you furnish the buyers with American Kennel Club applications for registra-
    tion _____
         Yes No

If No, please explain. _____

_____

_____

19. Are you connected *in any way* with a publication disseminating dog news or carrying dog advertising _____
    Yes, please give complete details on the attached GOLD SHEET. Yes No

20. Are you connected *in any way* with a dog food, dog remedy or kennel supply company _____ If Yes, please giv
    complete details on the attached GOLD SHEET. Yes No

21. Have you ever been suspended from the privileges of The American Kennel Club _____
    Yes No

    If so, state the date and circumstances _____

    _____

    _____

    _____

    _____

    _____

I hereby submit this application to the Board of Directors of the American Kennel Club for their consideration ar
make the following representations:

That I am not occupationally ineligible to judge under the provisions of Chapter 10, Section 1 (Dog Show rules) whic
reads: "Any reputable person who is in good standing with The American Kennel Club may apply for leave to judg
any breed or breeds of pure-bred dogs which in his or her opinion he or she is qualified by training and experience
pass upon, with the exception of persons connected with any publication in the capacity of solicitor for kennel adve
tisements, persons connected with dog food, dog remedy or kennel supply companies in the capacity of solicitor
salesman, persons employed in and about kennels, persons who buy, sell and in any way trade or traffic in dogs as
means of livelihood in whole or in part, whether or not they be known as dealers."

That I will at all times judge in accord with the current official standards and in strict conformity with the applicab
dog show rules, regulations and ring procedures as are in force at the time of the dog show that I am judging.

Marital Status _____

Name of Spouse _____

Date _____   _____
                                                      Signature of Applicant

(over)

Under current policy, a person eligible to be approved to judge one or more breeds at AKC licensed or member shows is also approvable to judge Junior Showmanship. If this application is approved for the breed or breeds for which you have applied, do you wish to have your name added to our list of judges eligible to be approved to judge Junior Showmanship

Yes _____ No _____

QUESTIONNAIRE FOR PROVISIONAL JUDGING APPLICANTS

READ INSTRUCTIONS CAREFULLY (Please Typewrite)

Under current policy, provisional applicants are required to meet with a representative of AKC for personal interview which must take place at least two (2) months prior to the Board meeting at whic their application will be presented.

Shortly after the receipt of your application, you will be notified as to the dates of your interview, th publication of your name in the Gazette, and the Board meeting at which your application will be sul mitted. If you have any questions, feel free to contact the Judges Department .

NAME _____ PHONE _____

ADDRESS _____

LIST BREED(S) APPLYING FOR:

1)   Explain how you became involved in the sport of dogs.

_____

_____

_____

_____

2)   Briefly explain why you believe you have amassed enough knowledge to become a competent dog sho judge.

_____

_____

_____

_____

_____

_____

) When did you start showing dogs? _____ (Year) _____

What breed(s) did you begin with? _____
                                          (Yes/No)   (Breeds)

Did you breed and register litters of that breed?_____If yes, indicate number of litters in each
                                                  (Yes/No)

breed. _____

) Since you began exhibiting at how many shows have you exhibited on a yearly basis? _____
                                                                               (Number)

Did you do your own handling?_____

If NO, explain and indicate who handled your dogs.

_____

_____

_____

_____

) How many shows other than those where you exhibit dogs do you attend on a yearly basis? _____
                                                                                        (Number)

) List at least five shows where you have observed the breed(s) for which you are applying being judged.

_____

_____

_____

_____

_____

) Different judges interpret a breed standard differently, and since judging is by its nature a subjective
   endeavor that requires an individual to develop a clear picture of the breed they want to judge, briefly explain the "type" you prefer in each of the breeds you have applied for.

_____

_____

_____

_____

_____

_____

_____

8) List several dogs, not necessarily now being shown that exemplify the type you described in question #7

_____

_____

_____

_____

9) List stewarding assignments you have had indicating show, date, breed (s) and judge (s).

_____

_____

_____

_____

10) List sweepstakes or futurities you have judged indicating club, date, and breed (s).

_____

_____

_____

_____

_____

_____

For each assignment, briefly describe the quality of competition.

_____

_____

_____

_____

_____

11) List match shows you have judged indicating club, date, and breed (s).

_____

_____

_____

_____

_____

For each assignment, briefly describe the quality of competition.

_____

_____

_____

_____

_____

12) List the names and addresses of several judges, handlers, breeders or other knowledgeable fanciers with whom you have discussed the breed(s) applied for in general preparation for making application who can be contacted to attest to this fact.

_____

_____

_____

_____

_____

13) List any books you have read, seminars you have attended or other educational experience you have had in general preparation for applying for provisional judging status.

_____

_____

_____

_____

14) List all litters you have bred, indicating breed (s) and litter numbers.

_____

_____

_____

_____

_____

15) Since a mark of a knowledgeable fancier is their ability to evaluate a litter at an early age, briefly critique five of the above listed litters.

_____

_____

_____

_____

_____

_____

_____

_____

_____

_____

_____

16) How many dogs of your breeding did you exhibit? _____
(Number)

How many completed their championships? _____
(Number)

17) If you had a stud dog (s), how many litters did he produce?_____
(Number of dogs)   (Number of litters)

8) For how long have you been contemplating applying for judging approvability? Briefly explain.

_____

_____

_____

_____

19) What are your aspirations in the field of judging? In other words, how many breeds would you feel you would want to be approved to judge in the future?

_____

_____

_____

_____

_____

20) List any supplemental information that you feel will assist the Board of Directors in evaluating your application for provisional judging status.

_____

_____

_____

_____

_____

_____

21) List shows and dates over the next four months that you could attend for the purpose of a personal interview.

_____

_____

_____

_____

_____

_____

_____

CONDITIONS OF PROVISIONAL JUDGING STATUS

I fully understand that a personal interview with a representative designated by AKC will be required prior to the consideration of my application by the Board of Directors.

If granted provisional judging status I fully understand that my judging eligibility is conditional and, therefore, reviewable by AKC Board of Directors at any time subsequent to the date the status was initially granted. Upon review, AKC's Board of Directors may relieve me of continued judging eligibility under the Provisional Judging system.

Regular judging status will be accorded to only those provisional judges that adequately demonstrate their competence as a judge to the satisfaction of the Board of Directors through their provisional judging assignments.

I fully understand and stipulate that the Board's authorization to judge on a provisional basis in no way guarantees or infers eventual approval as a regular judge whose name would appear in AKC's publication, "Dog Show and Obedience Trial Judges."

_____   _____

Date   *Signature*

As you run down through the application, you will be constantly referring to your notebook, kennel records and other dog-related materials. Take time and think as you respond to the questions as succinctly and honestly as possible. A treatise is not necessary so try not to ramble on and on with disjointed statements.

After you have answered all questions on your scrap paper, put the application aside for a day or two. This gives you a chance to refresh your mind as you attempt to clear your brain. When you return to the papers after this brief intermission, reread your answers and try to imagine a stranger following your application. Does it make sense? Have you clearly answered all the questions? Are you comfortable with what you have written? If you said no to any of these questions, rework your replies until you are satisfied. If you said yes, then fill in the original form using a typewriter. If you do not type, find a friend who does.

Both the questionnaire and examination papers will require more deep thinking than the actual application. Spend a lot of time on these and be sure of your responses. Toss any replies that are less than perfect in the trash basket and do them over and over until you are comfortable with what you have written. Rely on your instincts to guide you over areas that seem impenetrable.

All essay questions should be worked and reworked. Do not be afraid to state what you honestly believe, but do not pad your reply with empty words. The breed standards are useful as a guide but should not be quoted word for word. Use your own thoughts and draw your own conclusions.

The Judges Written Examination, which you must pass with at least an eighty percent score, is filled with true and false, or multiple choice questions that need to be carefully read. It is important to keep in mind that the major reason for which initial applications are denied is because the applicants failed to pass this exam. So, by all means refer to the official rules for guidance. Don't just ask your friends for the correct answers. Remember that you are the person who is taking the test, the one who may be called upon to make similar decisions in the ring. Where will your friends be then?

With the completion of the application, written exam and questionnaire, together with all attached forms and sheets, you are ready to apply officially. Photocopy at least one entire set of your papers before you submit them and keep your copy in the notebook. Enter the date of submission on the upper right hand corner of the first page of your copy of the application. All original papers should be sent to the American Kennel Club in care of the Judges' Department.

Interview

The Kennel Club will review your application papers as expeditiously as it can. If all appears to be in order and you scored well on the written exam, you will receive a letter from the AKC setting up an appointment for a personal interview. If the place and time referred to in the letter is not convenient for you, or if something comes up during the interim, advise the AKC by phone and request another appointment.

The purpose of this pre-interviewing is to enable all parties involved to become acquainted with one another, to ascertain that the application is accurate in its content and to discover exactly how much the interviewee knows about the breed or breeds he is applying for approval to judge as a Provisional. This session will also afford the prospective judge the opportunity to ask any questions he may have concerning his next steps and to help him understand what is required of him throughout the entire process.

As soon as practicable after the interview, your name and breeds under application will be published in the *Gazette* under the title of Judging Applications—Provisional Judges. The publication of your name enables all members of the dog fancy to be apprised of your desire to become a judge and gives them the opportunity to write to the AKC expressing their opinion of your expertise and qualifications if they should desire to do so. Positive letters received are extremely favorable for the judge-applicant. Negative letters may require the Kennel Club to contact you and review all allegations made therein. Determination on the validity of any charges rests with the AKC.

After the interview, your application goes through a three-tiered evaluation procedure with the written recommendations of the interviewer. The first process involves a study by the Staff Committee, which is comprised of some of the AKC officers, department heads and rotating field representative. This Committee makes its recommendations and forwards the same to the Board's Judging Committee, consisting of three members of the Board. They then review all facts and data available to them and make a determination, which is forwarded to the Board of Directors with all appurtenant papers attached. The Board renders the final decision.

Provisional

After publication of your name and if all appears in order, the Board will render a decision on your status as a Provisional Judge. If you are approved as a Provisional you will receive notification of this by a letter from the AKC and at the same time be apprised of your responsibilities as a Provisional. When you have completed three Provisional assignments, write to the AKC informating them that you have done so, listing the three shows and their dates as well as your entry. Be sure to keep a copy of this letter for your files.

Upon receipt of this letter, your name will be resubmitted to the Board for final review on full judging status. If the Board's action is favorable, the Provisional status will be dropped and your name will be placed on the regular list of Dog Show Judges. If the Board finds otherwise, you may be required to complete additional Provisional assignments until such time as you are deemed capable in all respects of receiving full status.

As a Provisional you may accept any number of shows, and while serving in such capacity your name will appear on the premium list with an asterisk denoting your position. Once full status has been granted the symbol will no longer appear.

Provisional Observations

During the Provisional period, you will be observed by a field representative and/or official of the AKC (preferably by a different observer each time). Arrive at your ringside at least 15 minutes ahead of your scheduled starting time and look around for the AKC Representative. Chances are he will also be looking for you as he will want to have the opportunity to talk with you before you enter the ring. Each representative has his own system of observing and his own thoughts that he shares with Provisionals. As a guide, the following is an excerpt of some advice given by one observer, William M. Schmick, AKC Vice-President and former Field Representative:

". . . You'll be observed on your ring control, and by that we mean, are you able to take charge? Are you running the ring? For example, if you are there at five minutes of ten for your ten o'clock assignment and at five minutes after ten there are no dogs in the ring, are you still sitting waiting for the stewards to turn them up, or have you gone to the stewards and said: 'Where is the first Class?'

"They reply: 'Well, we're missing a dog.'

"You say: 'Where is the second class?'

"They say: 'That's a two dog class.'

" 'Well, are they both there? Fine, let's do the second class first.'

"In other words, are you a take charge person? Do you control your ring so that exhibitors know where you want them and what you want of them. Are they moving in the gaiting pattern you want them to move in, not the one they want? We're interested in your ring procedure and we don't care what it is as long as you have one and you stick to it. For an example, most judges (I would say 90% of all judges) will examine animal 'A' and they will move it and they form in their mind an opinion of whether they can use that one, or they can't use that one, or maybe they are going to have to use that one: three categories. Then they go to animal 'B' and they form the same judgment. Now, 10% of the judges will go examine dog 'A', then they will examine dog 'B', and then dog 'C' and then they will come back and they'll move dog 'A'. They'll move dog 'B', they'll move dog 'C'. In a big class that takes a computer mind, by the time number 13 is moving, to remember whether that was the one with the funny bite or not. It is quite a task. Whereas if you've used the former procedure, sorting them out as you went along in their totality, you follow a much more orderly system. But my point is, we're not going to switch you from that second system if that's what you are comfortable with and that's the way you want to judge. Maybe sometime we'd ask you to try it the other way once to see how you liked it. But if it's your procedure and you stick with it and that's fine.

"We're interested in your decisiveness and a clue to that, and only a clue, is how well you stick to a time schedule. For example, if you are only judging 12 or 15 dogs an hour, we wonder if you know what you are doing. If you do 40 dogs an hour, we wonder if you're giving exhibitors their $10.00 worth. On the other hand if when you start out judging you do 18 to 22 dogs an hour, fine, you'll get so you can do it more decisively when you've been judging for awhile.

"We are anxious to have you talk to exhibitors and ringside as little as possible before, during or after your assignment. There are so many amateurs and novices at ringside today who have an almost infinite capacity to misinterpret an innocent discussion between a judge and an exhibitor (I give a very hyperbolic example, but it makes the point): You have a woman who has gone Best of Winners and you say to her, 'Your dog is in lovely condition and moves so nicely today.'

"She says, 'Thank you very much. This win finished the dog!'

"Now that's a perfectly innocent discussion, but ringside thinks it went something like this: You said, 'See I told you at the dinner last night I would put you up.'

"She says: 'Yes, and your check will be in the mail on Monday morning.'

"Obviously such a thing has never happened, but when you have

42

discussion, you lay yourself open to the criticism that something very untoward like that might have been what was being discussed.

"You're going to get people who will say, 'What didn't you like about my little Suzie?' And the answer to that is, 'If you will bring Suzie back later this afternoon, after I'd had my luncheon and so forth, we'll go out into the parking lot and I will discuss little Suzie with you. But you must remember that the other six dogs in the class will not be there for a comparison.' She will, in most instances, not come back because she doesn't really care about what you didn't like about Suzie. She wants to tell you you don't know how to judge. And the minute you try to give her an objective analysis and say, 'I would like to see her move a little better behind.' She will say, 'Well, twelve judges have told me this is the best moving dog they've ever seen.' Or you say, 'The head is a little heavy for me.' She will respond, 'Well Alva Rosenberg said it was the best head on any Shih Tzu he'd ever seen.' So, it's an exercise in futility to be avoided if you possibly can.

"Last but not least, if you have any problems at all, don't hesitate to call for the AKC Representative or the Superintendent, now or ten years from now. It is always better to ask a stupid question than to make a stupid mistake. I will try to come back and watch you judge at some point. If I have any comments, I'll get with you at the end of your assignment and if I don't, you'll know I had nothing to suggest to you."

You will obviously be very nervous and trying your darnedest to hide your emotions as you clutch your hands behind your back, in your pockets, or to your thighs, hoping the AKC does not notice that you are shaking like a leaf on a windy day. This is a perfectly normal reaction to the situation. Even as you enter the ring, begin judging for the first time, you may be all thumbs as you swiftly try to recall just what it is that you are supposed to do, how it should be done and why you're doing it. While in the recesses of your mind, you are aware that someplace Godfather is watching you, scrutinizing every move you make. You may be asking yourself: Will he approve? Am I doing it right? Oh, God, why did I ever get into this mess? Relax. Take a deep breath. Forget about anything and everyone except the dogs in the ring.

It is important to realize that the Observer is not there to agree with your decisions, but rather on your ability to be consistent in choosing type, have correct ring procedure and control and whether or not you look like you know what you are doing. In short, you need to have the aura and bearing of a judge.

If you have the potential makings of a good judge, you will quickly settle down and forget about anyone watching you judge and judging you in turn whether this be an official, exhibitor or unknown ringside spectator. Some obscure element envelopes you as if you entered another world. Your consciousness centers on the dogs, and secondarily on the people holding the other end of the leads. Only after you have appraised your last dog, marked the book, handed out the final ribbon, posed for the BOB picture and stepped out of your ring will you reenter the here and now.

After completion of the assignment, you should look around for the Representative as you head for the Superintendent's desk to hand in your book. You may have questions for him or he may have a few thoughts he wants to share with you. If he does, accept his comments gracefully as he is only trying to help you. Do not argue, even if you disagree vehemently with what he says. Likewise, don't become flustered, backing away from a decision which you feel was justified. Stand your ground, but be open enough to learn. Take the words in their proper context and do not insert your own personal thoughts. If you can accept criticism gracefully and at face value, you should be able to advance yourself from the ordeal.

If your Provisionals have gone well, you will receive approval from the Board of Directors elevating your status to that of a regular judge and your name will be published in the *Gazette* denoting this fact. Surely this is a time to celebrate, but too often the felicitious letter is anticlimatic when you consider all you went through to garner such an auspicious title. Chances are you will merely breathe a sigh of relief and begin thinking about additional breeds.

Paperwork surrounds the Board's Committees.
Harding—GAZETTE, American Kennel Club

3

Applying for
Additional Breeds

YOU HAVE BEEN BITTEN BY THE BUG and discovered that
it suits you well. You like judging, appreciate the challenge and are
able to rise to the occasion. It is natural for you to want to increase
your judging experiences by seeking other breeds and larger entries.
The only way you can accomplish this feat is to apply for additional
breeds. But, are you ready? What breeds or how many can you go
for? And, are you going to get them?

There is no simple answer to those questions. What may apply to
one, does not necessarily apply to all as the subject of additional
breeds leaves itself open to vast interpretations. Nevertheless, let's
take a look at the system as it exists today.

What to Apply For

A judge who is pursuing the approval for additional breeds should
not venture forth lightly. Instead, he had best prepare himself to meet
all the struggles he will face. No longer can one just make application
after application, hoping to wear the Board down by sheer obstinacy.
Also, the minute new breeds are granted, one cannot return with
forms requesting other breeds. Fortunately or unfortunately (depend-

ing on one's point of view), the granting of additional breeds is based on more than just who you know, but what you know as well.

Since the entire judging process takes a considerable length of time, it is not wrong for you to begin thinking of different breeds as soon as you have received full judging status. Indeed those who have mapped out their plans in advance, established short and long term goals and laid a straight path are less apt to be faced with detours. So, if you really like judging and wish to pursue it further, then you must begin thinking of the future.

Generally it is advisable for one to complete a group before seeking breeds from different groups. The reason for this is that in obtaining assignments, clubs tend to keep their judges within a group, rather than skipping around.

If you are a new judge and have approval for but one or two breeds, consider related breeds as your next step. In other words, if you are approved for English Setters, don't go after Beagles. Instead pursue Irish or Gordon Setters and continue on in degrees until you have the Sporting Group if that is your ultimate goal. However, if you really wish to judge only occasionally (once or twice a year) and want to maintain an active breeding and showing program for the next ten years or so, do feel free to skip around and go after whatever breeds you feel you have the background and knowledge to sustain in any group regardless of their relationship to your original approved breeds.

Under the assumption that you are like a majority of our judges and want as many breeds as is conceivable, you must keep your ultimate goal constantly in mind. If you would like eventually to become a group judge, begin now by studying all breeds within that group. Not only should you read any resource material available, but you need to observe those breeds at shows, watch the judging, talk to breeders and try to get a handle on the breed or breeds. Accept as many match shows as you can for the group you are interested in pursuing. Use your experiences to learn continually about the breeds in question. Education is the best preparation you can acquire to assist you in achieving your goals.

As a single or two-breed judge, you have had little actual judging experience at point shows. Therefore, you must also increase your knowledge about ring procedure and control. To accomplish this, you need to practice and observe, talk with other judges and learn about the peculiar little occurrences that can happen and how they should be handled.

In short, just because you are currently an approved judge you cannot just sit back on your laurels. Rather you need to be continuously reading, observing and listening. Do not go only to shows where you judge, nor to those where you show your dogs and leave soon afterwards. Instead, attend shows with the sole purpose of furthering your education by encouraging the development of your eye and augmenting your knowledge. Having prepared yourself, you should be in good condition to apply for additional breeds.

But what breeds? That has to be a leading question. We all want as much as we can get and very few of us will always get what we want. Therefore it is a wise person who carefully assesses the situation, makes note of his weaknesses and strengths and apprises himself of the prevailing winds and current patterns. If the AKC has not been granting ten or fifteen breeds at a clip, do not waste your time or its in applying for that many. Rather look for the related breeds, key breeds and those for which you can attest vast knowledge.

If the AKC considers you group material, they will grant you all of your "wrap-up" breeds if you are approaching full group status and apply for them all. On the other hand, if you are currently approved for one group and wish to venture into another group, you must be satisfied with going slowly.

Once you have a rough idea of the direction you are heading in and the breeds you would like, call or write to the AKC and request an appointment to discuss your future. Make the trip to New York, or try to have the meeting scheduled at a show in your area, being prepared to put some mileage on the car if necessary. Your best bet is to talk with someone who has had the opportunity to review your file and has an understanding of the situation. You should look for advice on advancement: if you are pursuing the right breeds, too many or too little; and to give you general assistance and answer any questions.

Remember the path to achieving additional breeds is not an easy one, and is at times frustrating. However, if you carefully assess the "modus operandi," being aware of current trends and act accordingly, you will proceed down the road at a quicker pace than if you tried to take shortcuts and found yourself stymied.

When to Apply

There is no precise timetable to guide you in calculating the right time to apply. In a letter from the AKC to additional breed applicants, the matter is approached as follows:

"A central factor in the consideration of any application for additional breeds is the judge's overall exposure in his or her most recently approved breeds. Simply put, the Board wants to see that judges have judged their last approved breeds enough to gain confidence and proficiency in the breed(s) in question. Although no precise number of assignments is 'required', it can be said that additional breeds will ordinarily not be granted to any applicant who has not judged his or her most recently approved breed(s) four or five times. It is important in this context to realize that the Board will expect to see more exposure in breeds that draw large and therefore more difficult entries. That is to say, so called 'key breeds' should be judged numerous times before an application for additional breeds is filed."

In personal terms, it is best to only apply for additional breeds when you feel you are thoroughly comfortable with the breeds currently approved, have done sufficient homework for the new breeds and feel the time is right.

The Application

To procure the necessary forms for additional breeds, write a letter to the AKC in care of the Judges' Department requesting all material pertaining to the application for additional breeds. See the following pages for copies of the papers you should receive in a response to your request:

The Application to Judge Additional Breeds is very similar to your first application to judge. Most of the questions are identical and those that are not refer to your judging experiences.

The Questionnaire differs from the one you filed in your quest for initial approval in that it deals solely with questions concerning breeds under application at this time.

In the near future the AKC will combine the above two forms into one all-inclusive application/questionnaire.

When filling out your forms for additional breeds, you should follow the same steps as you did when you initially applied: answer all questions on scrap paper first, making as many drafts as necessary. By this time, if you have been diligently keeping track of your activities, your notebook should be crammed with information regarding your past experiences as a judge, observations made in studying

THE AMERICAN KENNEL CLUB
51 MADISON AVENUE
NEW YORK, N.Y. 10010

Dear Additional Breed Applicant:

Under the present system for considering applications for additional breeds, the Board of Directors of The American Kennel Club has decided that a personal interview with the applicant is desirable. This procedure is intended to provide a twofold benefit.

First, AKC wants to get to know applicants for additional breeds as well as is possible before the Board considers their applications. Second, it is our belief that applicants for additional breeds are often confused as to the criteria employed by the Board in determining who should be granted additional breeds and how many breeds should be granted. By providing applicants with an opportunity to discuss their applications with a representative designated by the Board, it is our hope that all judges will gain a better understanding of AKC procedures and concerns in this critical area.

Before filling out the questionnaire and application that accompanies this letter, the Board asks all applicants to give serious consideration to the following points:

A central factor in the consideration of applications for additional breeds is the judges' overall exposure in their most recently approved breeds. Simply put, the Board wants to see that judges have judged their last approved breed(s) enough to gain confidence and proficiency in the breed(s) in quesiton. It can be said that ordinarily _additional breeds will not be granted to applicants who have not judged their most recently approved breed(s) at least five times_. It is important in this context to realize that the Board will expect to see more exposure in breeds that draw large and therefore more difficult entries. That is to say, so-called "key breeds" should be judged numerous times before an application for additional breeds is filed.

A common question of additional breed applicants is what specific criteria other than exposure in their most recently approved breeds are evaluated by the Board. Perhaps the most emphasis is placed on reports from our field representatives. As most of you are aware, AKC field representatives cover virtually every all-breed show in the Continental United States and an ever increasing percentage of all independent specialties. At shows, field representatives observe judges to see whether or not the judges have a ring presence that produces the feeling that they are at ease judging their assignments. Procedure and control are observed to see that a judge goes about the business of judging in an orderly manner. Particular attention is placed on the judge's ability to consistently select breed type. It should be understood that field representatives do not pass judgement on the judge's placements, but, rather, are interested in a judge's ability to pick and stick with a particular type of dog. This is, of course, presuming that judges have sufficient quality of a particular type to make the consistent selection of type possible.

In addition to the foregoing, a comprehensive review of the judge's entire file is made. All information in a judge's file is carefully evaluated. The Board is particularly interested in the applicant's overall background in dogs. Decisions to advance or not to advance judges are not arbitrary. Applicants are considered on their own merits after a thorough review of their judge's file and record has been completed.

Instructional letter accompanying the additional Breed Application

The American Kennel Club knows that the continued development of the present equitable and flexible judging system is imperative. We believe the procedure of interviewing applicants is a large step in the right direction. However, it should not be viewed as a panacea. In many senses, Judging presents a paradox. Many fanciers, principally judges, feel AKC is entirely too conservative in granting additional breeds. On the other hand, there are many fanciers, probably the overwhelming majority of all exhibitors, who believe that AKC has been far too liberal in the approval of additional breeds. AKC is certainly cognizant of both views and has attempted to follow a policy of moderation that provides judges with an opportunity to get additional breeds while at the same time protecting the right of exhibitors to have experienced and knowledgeable judges judging assignments. We will continue this policy and feel certain that the procedure of interviewing prospective applicants for additional breeds before the Board considers their applications will provide another dimension that will enhance the overall process.

As mentioned above, AKC will be given an unprecedented opportunity to discuss with each judge his or her goals and aspirations in the judging world. This can only produce a healthy atmosphere as AKC will be able to broaden its base of information on applicants for additional breeds, and, as we all know, the more information that is available, the more educated the decisions predicated on this information will be.

Should you have any questions concerning this matter, please do not hesitate to write or call the Judges Department. Thank you for your cooperation in this matter.

THE AMERICAN KENNEL CLUB

attachment
H-80A

AMERICAN KENNEL CLUB • 51 Madison Avenue, New York, N. Y. 10010

APPLICATION TO JUDGE ADDITIONAL BREEDS

List in order of preference/experience breed(s) applying for _____

_____

_____

_____

_____

Name (Print) _____ Home Phone _____

Complete Home Address (including zip code) _____

_____ Date of Birth _____

Do you have any physical handicaps? _____ If "Yes", describe them _____
Yes or No

_____

_____

Business, Profession or Occupation _____

Title of your position or description of what you do _____

_____

Company Name (or "self-employed") _____

Business Address_____Business Phone_____
              (Street)

_____
   (City or Town)   (State)   (Zip Code)

Are you connected in any way with a publication disseminating dog news or carrying dog advertising? _____
                                         Yes or No

If "Yes", please give the information requested on the attached **WHITE** sheet.

Are you connected in any way with a dog food, dog remedy or kennel supply company? _____
                                         Yes or No

If "Yes", name the company and describe in detail your activities on the attached **WHITE** sheet.

Do you reside in the same household with or are you a member of the immediate family of a professional handler?

_____ If "Yes", give handler's name _____
Yes or No

Do you maintain a breeding kennel? _____Give name of breed (s), location, and length
                                Yes or No

of time operated _____

_____

_____

_____

To what extent, if any, do you board dogs for others? _____

_____

_____

Do you groom, condition, prepare for the show ring or train dogs belonging to others? _____
                                                                                      Yes or No

If "Yes", give details _____

_____

_____

_____

Do you co-own any dogs? _____ If "Yes", give the information requested on attached **WHITE** sheet.
                         Yes or No

Do you buy dogs for resale? _____ Do you buy dogs to improve your breeding stock? _____
                            Yes or No   Yes or No

Do you regularly or occasionally take dogs belonging to others into the show ring? _____
                                                                                   Yes or No

Have you bred any litters of the breed (s) applied for? _____ If "Yes", give breed (s) and
                                                        Yes or No

AKC litter numbers _____

_____

_____

If you have owned one or more dogs of the breed (s) applied for, give the registered names of the dogs and length of time

owned _____

_____

_____

If you have not bred or owned any of the breeds applied for, what other background do you have in these breeds? Please use
the attached **YELLOW** sheet to detail such background.

Do you make any charge for your services as a judge over and above your expenses? _____
                                                                                   Yes or No

I hereby submit this application to the Board of Directors of The American Kennel Club for their consideration and make the
following representations:

That I am occupationally eligible to judge under AKC dog show rules (Chapter 10, Section 1): "Any reputable person who is in
good standing with The American Kennel Club may apply for leave to judge any breed or breeds or pure-bred-dogs which in his
or her opinion he or she is qualified by training and experience to pass upon, with the exception of persons connected with any
publication in the capacity of solicitor for kennel advertisements, persons connected with dog food, dog remedy or kennel
supply companies in the capacity of solicitor or salesman, persons employed in and about kennels, persons who buy, sell and
in any way trade or traffic in dogs as a means of livelihood in whole or in part, whether or not they be known as dealers."

That I will at all times judge in accord with the current approved standards and in strict conformity with the applicable dog
show rules, regulations and ring procedures as are in force at the time of the dog show that I am judging.

Marital Status _____

Name of Spouse _____

Date _____
                                        Signature of Applicant

Please give the information requested on the attached **BLUE** sheet, which is part of the application.

If you are connected in any way with a publication disseminating dog news or carrying dog advertising, please name the publication, its complete address, your position and describe in detail your duties and activities.

If you are connected in any way with a dog food or kennel supply company, please give its name, complete address, your position and describe in detail your duties and activities.

you co-own any dogs?_____If "Yes" give the information requested below.
                    Yes or No

ed	Registered Name	Name of Co-Owner
_____	_____	_____
_____	_____	_____
_____	_____	_____
_____	_____	_____
_____	_____	_____
_____	_____	_____
_____	_____	_____
_____	_____	_____
_____	_____	_____
_____	_____	_____

Please describe the experience, other than breeding, you have had in the breeds applied for. If you have had an opportunity to judge any of the breeds applied for at sanctioned matches, sweepstakes or futurities make indication below, giving the name and the date of the event.

Please indicate assignments you are scheduled to judge within the next six months giving the show, the date and the breeds assigned.

List the shows in which you have exhibited dogs of any breed during the last 3 years.

Breed	Dog's Name	Show & Year	Did you Personally Han
			Yes or No
_____	_____	_____	_____
_____	_____	_____	_____
_____	_____	_____	_____
_____	_____	_____	_____
_____	_____	_____	_____
_____	_____	_____	_____
_____	_____	_____	_____
_____	_____	_____	_____
_____	_____	_____	_____
_____	_____	_____	_____

Have you judged sanctioned matches in the past 3 years?_____If "Yes", list names of clubs
Yes or No

holding the matches and dates of them_____

_____

_____

_____

_____

_____

_____

_____

_____

Do you have any active membership in dog clubs?_____If "Yes", list them and state if yo
Yes or No
have ever held office.

Club	Office	In What Years Did you hold Office
_____	_____	_____
_____	_____	_____
_____	_____	_____
_____	_____	_____

THE AMERICAN KENNEL CLUB
51 Madison Avenue
New York, N.Y. 10010

QUESTIONNAIRE FOR ADDITIONAL BREEDS
(please type)

READ INSTRUCTIONS CAREFULLY

This questionnaire must be completed in full. Answers should be brief, yet informative. However, should additional space be required to answer any question, please use 8½ x 11 paper. Be sure to clearly indicate the question that is being answered on supplemental sheets of paper.

Please be advised that you should have a minimum of five (5) assignments in each of your most recently approved breeds.

If this requirement is met, your name together with the breeds for which you are applying will be published in the first available issue of the Gazette. Three (3) months following publication, your application will be submitted to our Board of Directors for consideration. You will be notified of the dates of publication and Board consideration shortly after your application is received.

NAME _____ PHONE _____

ADDRESS _____

List in order of preference/experience breed applying for. _____

_____

_____

1. Give a brief general explanation of why you are applying for additional breeds to judge. _____

_____

_____

_____

_____

For each breed applied for, indicate the reason you are applying for that breed together with an explanation of your general background in the breed. _____

_____

_____

_____

_____

3. If you have owned, exhibited or bred any of the breeds applied for, indicate the registered name and number of each dog owned, the year(s) you owned the dog, when you first exhibited the breed and the number of litters (specifying litter numbers) of the breed you have bred.

BREED	DOG'S NAME & REGISTERED NO.	YEARS OWNED/EXHIBITED

BREED	YR. LITTER WHELPED	LITTER NO.

4. List the names and addresses of several judges, handlers, breeders or other knowledgeable fanciers with whom you have discussed the breed(s) applied for in general preparation for making application who can be contacted to attest to this fact.

5. List some of the shows over the last five years where you have observed the breed(s) applied for being judged. _____

_____
_____
_____
_____
_____
_____
_____
_____
_____
_____

6. List any books and/or articles you have read or seminars you have attended in general preparation for making application for approval to judge the breed(s) in question. _____

_____
_____
_____
_____

State your eventual goals and aspirations in the field of judging in general as well as specific terms. In other words, how many breeds you would want to be approved to judge eventually. If there has been a change in this regard since your last application, please explain. _____

_____
_____
_____
_____

_____

_____

_____

_____

8. List the show, date and entry for each assignment you have judged in your last breeds approved together with a brief explanation of the quality of the competition at each assignment. _____

_____

_____

_____

_____

_____

_____

_____

_____

_____

_____

9. List show and date for any future assignment(s) over the next four months, and indicate with an asterisk (those in your most recently approved breeds.

_____

_____

_____

_____

_____

_____

_____

List shows and dates over the next four (4) months that you could attend for the purpose of a personal interview.

_____

_____

_____

_____

_____

_____

_____

_____

_____

Have you ever judged the breed(s) applied for at match shows (fun or sanctioned), sweepstakes or futurities?_____ If yes, list the name of the club, date and entry. _____
yes/no

_____

_____

_____

_____

_____

Give a general explanation of the breed type you prefer in the breed(s) applied for. _____

_____

_____

_____

_____

_____

_____

_____

_____

13. Select several dogs over the years in the breed(s) applied for *not necessarily being shown currently* exemplify the type you prefer in the breed(s). Feel free to critique these dogs pointing out attributes b good and bad that you have observed.

BREED	DOG'S NAME	YEARS EXHIBIT
		(approximate)

14. Do you belong to any specialty clubs for the breed(s) applied for?_____
                                                                        yes/no

CLUB	YEARS OF MEMBERSHIP	POSITIC (IF A

eel free to give any information not asked for in this questionnaire that you believe supplements your ackground in dogs in general and the breed(s) you have applied for in particular. _____

_____

_____

_____

_____

_____

_____

I understand that the Board of Directors may feel that a personal interview with one or more representatives signated by the Board may be required before my application is given final consideration. I further understand at my additional breed application will not be processed unless this questionnaire is completed in full.

_____
Signature

ate _____

dogs and talking with breeders concerning the new breeds you wish to seek and various other bits and pieces of data accumulated. This material will provide you with valuable source information to draw from in answering some of the questions.

When you have completed your draft responses, lay everything aside for a few days. After this interval, go back and reread your answers for clarity and conciseness. If you are satisfied, type them on the original forms (or have someone type for you), using extra sheets of heavy bond blank white paper, if necessary, photocopy the entire proceeding for your files and send the originals to the AKC.

Your name and all additional breeds applied for will then be published in the *Gazette* to give members of the fancy an opportunity to write pro or con letters regarding your eligibility to adjudicate those breeds.

The Interview

The personal interview for additional breeds is not an undertaking that many judges relish, but one for which they must prepare in advance. Giving ample preparation time, you will receive notification for the AKC advising you of the date and time of the interview and name of your interviewer. If you have a particular problem with the scheduled date and time, contact the AKC and request an alternative.

As you will see from this sample letter, you are not only apprised of the interview, but also the month in which the Board will pass on the Application and additional information requested.

The night before the interview, review your notebooks, application, questionnaire and standards for the breed or breeds under consideration.

When you talk with the interviewer, try to be calm, courteous and concise in your oral responses. The session should go well if you are strong without appearing arrogant, courteous without being too solicitous and knowledgeable but not overbearing.

Following the interview, the interviewer will file his report with the AKC indicating his findings. A favorable report is, of course, a plus but not a guarantee, just as one that is unfavorable is not totally deterrent to your cause.

THE AMERICAN KENNEL CLUB
51 MADISON AVENUE
NEW YORK, N.Y. 10010

We are in receipt of your application to judge additional breeds, and the list below indicates the next steps in processing your application. Please refer to the item(s) marked with an "X" preceding it.

_____Your name together with the breeds for which you are applying will be published in the _____issue of the Gazette. Accordingly, your application has been scheduled for the _____Board meeting.

_____In accordance with the above, an interview has been arranged at the following location with the interviewer so named. (If at a show, please contact the interviewer at the Superintendent's desk to arrange a mutually convenient time for the interview).

If you cannot keep the above interview date, please advise immediately as your application may be rescheduled for a later Board meeting depending on the date of the actual interview.

_____Please send your Additional Breed Application at your earliest convenience. (Applications received less than one (1) month prior to the above Board meeting may result in the rescheduling of your application for the following month.)

_____Your application is incomplete. Please answer or further explain, which ever applicable, question(s).

If you have any questions, please do not hesitate to contact me.

Very truly yours,

JUDGES DEPARTMENT

NOTE: YOU WILL BE NOTIFIED VIA LETTER OF THE BOARD'S ACTION ON YOUR APPLICATION. LETTERS WILL BE MAILED THE DAY FOLLOWING THE BOARD MEETING (INDICATED ABOVE). PLEASE DO NOT CALL AKC REGARDING THE BOARD'S ACTION AS THIS INFORMATION WILL NOT BE GIVEN OVER THE TELEPHONE.

Interview letter

Following the designated Board meeting, you will receive a letter from the AKC stating whether or not you were approved for the additional breed or breeds. It is possible to receive a positive nod for only some of the breeds applied for, in which case you will be either content to have received something or upset because you did not get everything.

Application All or Partially Denied

If you should be turned down for all or even some of the breeds you applied for, your initial reaction will be one of hurt and anger. This is to be expected for a denial is a personal matter and represents the AKC saying that you do not have the knowledge to adjudicate that breed or breeds. What should you do?

First of all vent your anger and frustration. Don't call your friends, lambasting the system, but rather engage in some sort of physical exercise, or go to a movie—anything to clear the air enough to enable you to think rationally. Ask yourself three questions: Did I do all my homework? Did I deserve that breed? Would I have been able to judge it and judge it correctly? If you responded no, then go back and start over again. Chances are that with more knowledge and ability you should receive approval the next time around.

If you said yes and truly believe you were wronged, what should you do? Well, there are two avenues of recourse available:

1) Call the AKC and request an appointment to sit down and discuss the matter. Ask to have your file pulled and be given an honest and frank appraisal of why the Board reasoned as it did. Seek answers that are justifiable and direct. If there has been a misunderstanding, seize this opportunity to straighten it out.

2) If this appointment did not satisfy you, apply for an appeal of the Board's decision. A Review Board, consisting of two members of the Board of Directors who did not sit in on the meeting where your application was discussed and voted, is in existence. Go before the Review Board with all supporting data to assist you in substantiating your case. Ask to have your file present and request definite reasons why you were denied.

4

Handling Assignments

O NE PROBLEM all judges must contend with is in establishing an easy yet precise system of handling assignments, correspondence and calendars.

Match Shows

Match shows present the least problem to the judge as they are informally run with no restrictions as to breeds, number of dogs exhibited or distance between shows. As a potential judge, your match show assignment requests usually come through recommendations by friends or friends of friends who are aware of your judging aspirations.

An inquiry at a show, or a phone call asking your availability is all that is initially required. However, this inquiry should be followed up with a brief letter stating your assignment, date and location of the show. The Show Chairman's name, address and telephone number should also be included. Match show judges are not paid or reimbursed for their expenses, but many clubs do give them a gift as a token of their appreciation.

Hopefully, you will receive a copy or two of the flyer, which lists all pertinent show information (including directions) at least three weeks prior to the date of the show. It is not uncommon for the judge to be the last to receive this data and the flyer may arrive as late as a day or two before the show. If you do not receive the information promptly, you should telephone the chairman to ascertain the status of the show and your participation in it. Sometimes match shows are calamitous, which makes it imperative that you be flexible.

Point Shows

Out of necessity point shows are run differently. Here everyone has to know just what is expected of him. Judges need to handle all their show contacts as if they were dealing with a business, or as some say, a bureaucratic maze. Careful and concise records must be kept of all past, present and future assignments to avoid errors and confusion.

Most of your initial contacts from show-giving clubs will be either in person or by phone, and should always be followed up in writing. Personal contacts generally take place at a show where you may be judging, exhibiting or attending as a spectator. The show's chairman or a member of the judge's committee will ask you if you are available for a particular show, specifying date, location and breeds under consideration. This inquiry may be an exchange to determine your availability and other particulars or may be regarded by the club as a firm commitment, especially if you say you do not have a conflict. Do not let any assignment stand on verbal discussion. Instead *insist* on a confirmation letter and only mark that show in your calendar as final when you have received such a letter. Some judges deal with in-person requests by carrying around a small pocket calendar in which they have noted their assignments. Still others tell the person inquiring that they are unsure of their schedule and ask for both a phone call and a letter. Many judges maintain that clubs should not make inquiries at shows as this leads to misunderstandings and inevitable snafus.

Phone Calls

The best way to make initial contact as to a judge's availability is by phoning. Phone calls can quickly apprise the querying club of three immediate factors:

1) Is he free to judge on that day?
2) Breeds available, and
3) Fee and/or expenses. The following is a sample telephone conversation:

CHAIRMAN: "Hello, Mr. Schneider. My name is Christian Johnson and I am show chairman for the Roosevelt Kennel Club in Hyde Park, New York. We are currently preparing our judging panel for next year's show. The date is May 20, 1981, and it will be held at the County Fairgrounds in Hyde Park. Would you be available to judge the Hound Group and all sight hounds?"

JUDGE: (Who on a notepad adjacent to the phone has been making note of the date and location of the show and breeds/group requested)—"Just a minute, let me check my calendar." (He quickly flips through his 1981 wall calendar to the month in question, sees that he is free for that day and checks for other shows that might conflict). "Yes, I'm available."

CHAIRMAN: "Good. What do you charge?"

JUDGE: "My fee is $100.00 plus expenses which includes transportation, lodging and meals."

CHAIRMAN: "That is fine with us."

JUDGE: "Would you please repeat your name and give me your telephone number, both at work and home, in case I have to contact you?"

CHAIRMAN: "Christian Johnson. Work number is 914-888-3333, Ext. 867 and home is 914-632-4489."

JUDGE: (He is writing this information on the notepad for later transfer to judging files)—"Thank you. Would you please send me a letter confirming the assignment?"

CHAIRMAN: "I'll get a letter out to you within the week."

JUDGE: "Good. Just so you are aware, I have a policy of keeping dates open for three weeks for clubs who make telephone inquiries. If I have not received a letter from you within that time, I will not hold the date if a subsequent confirmed assignment comes in."

CHAIRMAN: "That's OK. I'll see that you receive the confirmation letter as soon as possible and look forward to having you on our panel. Goodbye."

JUDGE: "It will be my pleasure, I'm sure. Goodbye."

For comprehension this sample represents a hypothetical, straightforward conversation. Phone calls do not always work that easily. Sometimes you will discover that you cannot judge that particular show because of a conflict with another show within the two hundred-mile, thirty-day restriction, or other restrictions placed on you by confirmed clubs. Perhaps the problem lies with being able to judge only some of the breeds requested. In this case, a shifting of breeds may be possible between yourself and another slated judge if the club is willing to make such changes, and so on. Some clubs may make a single call for both their show and a companion show, inquiring as to your availability for both shows and charges. In other words, telephone calls for querying have to be by their very nature flexible enough to encompass all probable conditions that may arise.

Occasionally calls are made at an inconvenient time. Midnight phone calls have to be the worst offenders as the proposed judge gropes through the darkness to consult his calendar while rubbing dreams out of his eyes. Sometimes, if he had not made note of the call, he may wake up the next morning with no recollection of even the ringing phone and hence has no idea of what transpired. Calls received during the cocktail hour or at a time when the judge may have overindulged are also likely to be soon forgotten. Therefore, it behooves all clubs to make every effort to contact their judges at hours that are considered as reasonable by most persons—on weekends, during the day or early evenings after dinner. Time zone differences have to be kept in mind if calls are made from one end of the country to the other. Judges who have young children, or spouses who want to have nothing to do with the whole business, should instruct their family members to restrict the message taking to the caller's name and telephone number for a return call. It is not unusual for a message to become so mixed up that it nowhere near resembles the actual words spoken.

Letters

If ever there is a nemesis in most judges lives, it has to exist in the one word ''correspondence.'' Unless you are fortunate enough to have a secretary or an understanding boss, you will become inundated with paperwork as your judging path progresses. All of which required your attention yesterday. It soon becomes a losing battle unless you can organize yourself to handle the load as expeditiously as possible. A rule of thumb is to reply to inquiries, reservation requests and what have you with the next mail. The longer paper sit around, needing to be taken care of, the more time you are apt to spend procrastinating.

Confirming and query letters from clubs form the bulk of your judging mail. The following is an example of a confirming letter:

ROOSEVELT KENNEL CLUB
Maple Street
Hyde Park, New York 12538

Date

Mr. John D. Schneider
2277 Valley Road
Bainbridge, Illinois 78906

Re: May '81 Show

Dear Mr. Schneider:

This letter confirms our telephone conversation of
yesterday regarding your availability to judge at our forthcoming 97th show to be held May 20, 1981, at the County
Fairgrounds in Hyde Park, New York. Your assignment
will be the Hound Group and all sight hounds (Afghan
Hounds, Borzoi, Greyhounds, Irish Wolfhounds, Salukis,
Scottish Deerhounds and Whippets). It is my understanding that your charge to our club will be $100.00 plus
expenses of transportation, lodging and meals. This is
agreeable with us.

Please sign the enclosed copy of this letter and return
the same to me in the stamped, self-addressed envelope. As
the show date approaches, our Hospitality Chairman will
be contacting you about transportation and motel
arrangements.

Looking forward to having you with us, I remain,

Very truly yours,
Christian Johnson
Show Chairman
Tel. #914-632-4489—Home
914-888-3333—Work

Upon receipt of this letter, you will recheck your calendar and files. If all appears to be in order and you do not have any conflicts, you will note final confirmation notation on the calendar, sign the copy of the letter and return it in the next mail to the show chairman. Your copy of the letter should be placed in your current assignment file (more on files later).

Some clubs will not ask you to sign and return a copy of the letter. I recommend that you do so anyhow so that both of you will have a complete record of the entire transaction. Make a photostatic copy of the club's letter. At the bottom of this copy, type "The above assignment is accepted in its entirety," date it and sign your name. Send this to the show chairman and note that you did so on the original which you keep in your files.

You may, of course, write your own separate letter of acceptance, but this is time consuming and not nearly as efficient as photocopying. Since this is a business arrangement, time is of the essence. Also there can be no question of your terms and agreements when you are dealing directly with the original contract, which in this case is the club's letter to you.

An inquiry letter means that a club wants to know if you will be available to judge on a specific data and what you will charge. This letter is not a contractual agreement but a preliminary correspondence that has been adopted by some clubs to ascertain two vital points:

1) if a particular judge is free and, in the case of multi-breed/group judges, those breeds/groups/BIS he would be able to officiate;

2) the approximate cost to the club for that particular judge's services.

There are occasionally problems with preliminary letters. Sometimes clubs word their letters in such a fashion that judges are made to feel that have been placed on the auction block with the assignment going to the lowest bidder. A club that is basically interested in dollars should invest in phone calls to their prospective judges to find out the upfront costs immediately. If he cannot afford a particular judge, the chairman should say so and not try to bargain for a lower amount.

Another difficult situation arises when judges are not subsequently informed by clubs if their services are desired or not. Very often judges will mark a query in their calendar and await further word. Unfortunately sometimes no other word comes, leaving the judge dangling without knowing whether or not he is on the panel.

Many specialty clubs use the query method to ascertain if already

70

nominated judges would be available or not. This enables them to poll their membership on only those judges who would be able to officiate at their event. It is helpful if the club secretary, when writing to prospective judges, would include some idea of a cut-off data at which time a judge is selected and advise the prospective judge that a follow-up letter will be sent letting him know whether or not he was chosen.

Some clubs do not use advanced calling. Instead they send out letters only to those individuals they would like on their panel and are not that concerned with running over their budget. A sample letter would be:

ROOSEVELT KENNEL CLUB
Maple Street
Hyde Park, New York 12538

Date

Mr. John D. Schneider
2277 Valley Road
Bainbridge, Illinois 78906

Dear Mr. Schneider: Re: May '81 Show

We would very much like to have you judge the Hound Group and the following breeds: Afghan Hounds, Borzoi, Greyhounds, Irish Wolfhounds, Salukis, Scottish Deerhounds and Whippets, at our spring show, which will be held on May 20, 1981, at the County Fairgrounds in Hyde Park, New York.

Would you please advise me by return mail if you are able to accept this assignment and what your fee to the club would be?

Looking forward to hearing from you, I remain,

Very truly yours,
Christian Johnson
Show Chairman

The judge who responds to this letter with a telephone call is making a mistake. Unless the conversation is recorded, there is no record of your contractual agreement. The telephone is useful if you have a particular problem, such as being able only to accept a portion of the assignment and want to discuss it with the show chairman. If changes are agreed to over the telephone, refer to the conversation and those changes in your responding letter.

Sometimes the onus is on the judge to be sure that the assignment is confirmed. You may receive a query letter from a club which you answer advising of your availability and charge, and then never hear anything further until you receive a copy of the premium list in the mail, which has you down to judge. This may or may not throw your into a tailspin—you could have conflicts, or made other plans for that day. Since you never received a final confirmation from the club, you assumed (rightly so) that you were not on the panel. Therefore, you should be prepared to undertake the burden of being sure that your assignments are properly confirmed. A sample letter would be as follows:

2277 Valley Road
Bainbridge, Illinois 78906
Date

Roosevelt Kennel Club
Mr. Christian Johnson
Maple Street
Hyde Park, New York 12538

Re: May '81 Show

Dear Mr. Johnson:

I have in my files a reply to your query letter regarding my availability to judge the Hound Group and Afghan Hounds, Borzoi, Greyhounds, Irish Wolfhounds, Salukis, Scottish Deerhounds and Whippets at your May 20, 1981, show, which will be held at the County Fairgrounds in Hyde Park, New York. I stated that my fee was $100.00 plus expenses of transportation, lodging and meals, and that I would be delighted to participate in your show.

As I have heard nothing further from you, would you please advise me whether or not I am on your panel. If I am, would you sign the enclosed copy of this letter and return the same to me in the stamped, self-addressed envelope so that I may have a final confirmation of this assignment for my files.

Best regards.

Very truly yours,
John D. Schneider

By enclosing a photostatic copy of your letter, you will make it easier for the harassed show chairman to respond to your letter and the self-addressed, stamped envelope serves as a reminder that you need final confirmation.

You may wonder why it is necessary for you to procure final confirmation. The primary reason is to avoid confusion and potential conflicts. If a judge is on record of requiring a final contractual agreement (and all judges should), he is in a better position to know just where he is going, when he is going to be there, what he is to judge and how much he is to receive for his efforts. As some clubs have maintained past performances of making their first letters to judges their final ones, many persons receive a big surprise to discover conflicts where conflicts were thought not to have existed. The ensuing result has been a waste of both time and money in phone calls to clubs and the AKC in an effort to straighten everything out. Such difficulties can be avoided by the practice of better business acumen by all parties involved.

It is not unusual for a club to sign up their judges two or more years in advance, which makes actual panel assignments difficult. All-breed and multi-group judges are contacted first as they are the busiest. The initial phone call or letter will be to ascertain availability and fee without getting into details about specific breeds, groups or best in show. In responding, these judges advise the club of their status regarding specific assignment. They need to commit the clubs as soon as possible and very often give a specified deadline for getting back to them with actual assignment. One all-breed judge, Henry H. Stoecker, has devised a quick method for advising inquiring clubs of his status via the use of his own assignment sheet. On this paper he blanks out all the boxes where he is in conflict, leaving open those breeds, groups and/or best in show for which he would be available to officiate at the inquirer's show. This sheet is then sent to the chairman in response to his query. The club marks the empty boxes that correspond with the actual assignment and returns the form to Mr. Stoecker, who in turn marks his calendar accordingly, notes the assignment on his master control sheets and files the sheet in its proper place. The master control sheets (which are identical to the assignment sheets except used for a different purpose) keep track of all his shows within the two hundred-mile, thirty-day limit—see new AKC restrictions for 1981 as covered later in this chapter and any other additional restrictions individual clubs may have placed on their judges, Each show is coded both by symbol and color and the respective assignments are so designated. Overlapping does occur when the sheets are filled to their capacity and new ones are used.

See the next two pages for a blank assignment sheet which can be readily adapted by most judges used in accordance with the breeds approved to judge and shows contracted.

Remuneration

Judges' remuneration, or the amount they receive for their expertise, time and expense, varies from judge to judge. Contrary to the opinions of some, the amounts charged are not picked out of a hat, nor are they computed in such a fashion as to make millionaires out of our judges. Indeed it has been stated by those who have tried that it is impossible to depend solely on the net income received from judging fees to make a living. What the net income does, however, is to supplement other monies received from a full or part-time job, investments, pensions and so on. It is necessary to remember that net income is different from gross income. Judges have many expenses that are not directly passed on to clubs, such as telephone, secretarial, office supplies, help at home while away, clothing and cleaning, travel expenses in attending shows for educational purposes, miscellaneous expenses occurred on the road while going to and from shows and so on. In otherwords, there are many costs which are not passed directly on to the clubs, but nevertheless are a direct result of a judging career or hobby.

(date)	(club)	(symbol)

_____

_____

_____

_____

☐ Best In Show
☐ Sporting Group
☐ Hound Group
☐ Working Group
☐ Terrier Group
☐ Toy Group
☐ Non-Sporting Group

SPORTING BREEDS
☐ Pointers
☐ Pointers (German Shorthaired)
☐ Pointers (German Wirehaired)
☐ Retrievers (Chesapeake Bay)
☐ Retrievers (Curly-Coated)
☐ Retrievers (Flat-Coated)
☐ Retrievers (Golden)
☐ Retrievers (Labrador)
☐ Setters (English)
☐ Setters (Gordon)
☐ Setters (Irish)
☐ Spaniels (American Water)
☐ Spaniels (Brittany)
☐ Spaniels (Clumber)
☐ Spaniels (Cocker)
☐ Spaniels (English Cocker)
☐ Spaniels (English Springer)
☐ Spaniels (Field)
☐ Spaniels (Irish Water)
☐ Spaniels (Sussex)
☐ Spaniels (Welsh Springer)
☐ Vizslas
☐ Weimaraners
☐ Wirehaired Pointing Griffons

HOUND BREEDS
☐ Afghan Hounds
☐ Basenjis
☐ Basset Hounds
☐ Beagles
☐ Black and Tan Coonhounds
☐ Bloodhounds
☐ Borzois
☐ Dachshunds
☐ Foxhounds (American)
☐ Foxhounds (English)
☐ Greyhounds
☐ Harriers
☐ Irish Wolfhounds
☐ Norwegian Elkhounds
☐ Otter Hounds
☐ Rhodesian Ridgebacks
☐ Salukis
☐ Scottish Deerhounds
☐ Whippets
☐ Ibizan Hounds

WORKING BREEDS
☐ Akitas
☐ Alaskan Malamutes
☐ **Bearded Collies**
☐ Belgian Malinois
☐ Belgian Sheepdogs
☐ Belgian Tervuren
☐ Bernese Mountain Dogs
☐ Bouviers des Flandres
☐ Boxers
☐ Briards
☐ Bullmastiffs
☐ Collies
☐ Doberman Pinschers

Henry Stoecker's assignment sheet which can
be easily adapted to suit any judge's needs.

- ☐ German Shepherd Dogs
- ☐ Giant Schnauzers
- ☐ Great Danes
- ☐ Great Pyrenees
- ☐ Komondorok
- ☐ Kuvaszok
- ☐ Mastiffs
- ☐ Newfoundlands
- ☐ Old English Sheepdogs
- ☐ Pulik
- ☐ Rottweilers
- ☐ St. Bernards
- ☐ Samoyeds
- ☐ Shetland Sheepdogs
- ☐ Siberian Huskies
- ☐ Standard Schnauzers
- ☐ Welsh Corgis (Cardigan)
- ☐ Welsh Corgis (Pembroke)

TOY BREEDS

- ☐ Affenpinschers
- ☐ Brussels Griffons
- ☐ Chihuahuas
- ☐ English Toy Spaniels
- ☐ Italian Greyhounds
- ☐ Japanese Spaniels
- ☐ Maltese
- ☐ Manchester Terriers (Toy)
- ☐ Miniature Pinschers
- ☐ Papillons
- ☐ Pekingese
- ☐ Pomeranians
- ☐ Poodles (Toy)
- ☐ Pugs
- ☐ Shih Tzu
- ☐ Silky Terriers
- ☐ Yorkshire Terriers

TERRIER BREEDS

- ☐ Airedale Terriers
- ☐ American Staffordshire Terriers
- ☐ Australian Terriers
- ☐ Bedlington Terriers
- ☐ Border Terriers
- ☐ Bull Terriers
- ☐ Cairn Terriers
- ☐ Dandie Dinmont Terriers
- ☐ Fox Terriers
- ☐ Irish Terriers
- ☐ Kerry Blue Terriers
- ☐ Lakeland Terriers
- ☐ Manchester Terriers (Standard)
- ☐ Miniature Schnauzers
- ☐ Norwich Terriers
- ☐ Scottish Terriers
- ☐ Sealyham Terriers
- ☐ Skye Terriers
- ☐ Soft-Coated Wheaten Terriers
- ☐ Staffordshire Bull Terriers
- ☐ Welsh Terriers
- ☐ West Highland White Terriers
- ☐ Norfolk Terriers

NON-SPORTING BREEDS

- ☐ Bichons Frises
- ☐ Boston Terriers
- ☐ Bulldogs
- ☐ Chow Chows
- ☐ Dalmatians
- ☐ French Bulldogs
- ☐ Keeshonden
- ☐ Lhasa Apsos
- ☐ Poodles
- ☐ Schipperkes
- ☐ Tibetan Terriers

- ☐ Miscellaneous Classes

Most judges compute their charges or fees to clubs in one of the following ways:

A) Flat fee, plus airfare if the distance involved from the judge's home to the show is such that airplane travel is required; otherwise, a straight flat fee with the judge paying for all expenses out of his pocket. Flat fees range from $200.00 up and are usually charged by group judges. Flat fees are usually the same for all shows, regardless of distances involved. Exceptions are made by some judges for independent specialty shows, where the fee may be reduced somewhat.

B) Flat fee, plus expenses consisting of transportation, lodging and meals. The flat fee is generally less than that which is quoted in "A", ranging from $50.00 to $175.00. Transportation means all expenses incurred while getting from home to the show grounds and back, via car, plane, train, bus, taxi or combination thereof. Car mileage is computed at the government figures for business. Meals are actual out-of-pocket expense for lunch, dinner and breakfast. The flat fee often covers all miscellaneous expenses.

Judges who are officiating at companion shows will split their expenses between the two shows, but charge full flat fees to each show. The advantage to the clubs is obvious as they each would be liable for one-half of a $400.00 plane fare, instead of the full $400.00.

C) Expenses only are charged by some judges and all AKC delegates. It is important to be definitive as to exactly what constitutes expenses. Besides transportation, lodging and meals, expenses may also include paying someone to dogsit or babysit, buying a new dress or visit to hairdressers, cleaning and so on, covering any and all costs that might arise. If first-class travel is part of the cost, be sure to apprise the club of that fact. Even without first-class air travel, expenses do have a way of adding up. Many clubs try to ascertain an exact dollar figure, and in responding to this request, judges need to be sure to allow for inflation and extra expense that may be incurred as a result of the location of the show. Some judges specify expenses "prevailing at the time of the show date." Motel rates are higher in and near a large city than out in the country. Resort areas tend to charge more. Therefore, it is difficult to project one's total costs for a given show and an additional padding of fifteen percent is not unexpected.

D) A dollar amount per dog is sometimes charged by newer judges who want to defray some of their expenses but realize they do not have enough breeds to warrant a higher cost for the club. This fee of $1.00 to $3.00 per dog is computed on the number of dogs actually entered under the respective judge. He then pays all of his expenses out of his own pocket. On some occasions he will make money on the transaction, but on others he will lose. Once in a while, a judge will charge so much a dog with a ceiling on the top figure. For an example, the judge computes in his mind the out-of-pocket expense for a show one hundred miles away, or approximately $115.00. As this is a large show and he is officiating over some of the key breeds in his group, he figures he may draw the maximum of 175 dogs. A fee of $2.00 a dog would bring his total charge to the club to $350.00. He may feel this is too much to ask, so he says he will charge $2.00 a dog with a top limit of $150.00, or on his contract he will state "$2.00 a dog or $150.00, whichever is less."

E) A specified sum contributed to the judge's favorite charity is a request made by some persons whose wealth is such that they do not mind absorbing all their expenses and will contribute their time and expertise for nothing. Nevertheless, these persons feel that it is not fair to other judges to make no monetary request at all and so opt for charitable donations in their name.

F) Gratis or the total sum of nothing is charged by some judges. Provisionals, brand new judges of a few breeds and club members who are officiating at their own show usually fall in this category. Other than these three categories, all judges should charge something to defray at least some of their expenses or as a recognition of their time and knowledge.

Restrictions

The AKC prohibits judges from accepting assignments over the same breeds, groups and/or best in show in events that lie within two hundred straightline miles of each other, regardless of terrain, and within thirty days at both ends—or thirty days prior to the show date and thirty days afterwards. For example, if you are already committed to judge Pekingese, Pomeranians and Silky Terriers at a show to be held on July 5, 1981, and receive an inquiry as to your availability to judge the exact same breeds at a show scheduled for August 3, 1981, which is situated within two hundred air miles of the July show, you would not be able to accept the later assignment. The same holds true if the second show was June 6, instead of August 3, and the request came after you were firmly committed to the July show. However, there are no restrictions over other breeds requests so that you would be able to judge Yorkshire Terriers and Shih Tzu at either show.

As we all know the American Kennel Club is constantly seeking ways to change and upgrade its procedures. Early in 1980 the AKC proposed a change in the area of judging restrictions. Plans were formulated to phase out in 1980 and '81 the thirty-day, two hundred-mile restriction referred to above in favor of a policy of dividing the country into zones and specified number of times a judge may officiate over a given breed, group or best in show within a zone in a six-month period by the calendar year of January 1 to June 30, and July 1 to December 31.

Just before this book went to press, William Stifel, President of the AKC, announced at the Delegates' Meeting on June 10, 1980 that the change had been rescinded. He advised the delegates that ample time would be given for comments if the AKC later reconsidered the proposed change.

For the readers' information, *if* the AKC should resubmit the change after this book is published, following is an excerpt from the report presented by Mr. Stifel at the Delegates' Annual Meeting on March 11, 1980 which spelled out the proposed plan. Underlined are the important aspects of the change the AKC then had in mind. If the AKC revives the plan, the details of it may be altered.

In 1979, your Board conducted a thorough review of the present *Judging Assignment Conflict Policy* and I would like to take a moment at this time to discuss a new policy on conflicts that will become effective January 1, 1981.

As you know, the present policy restricts judging assignments by time and distance. That is, a judge may not judge two assignments for the same competition that are within 30 days and 200 miles of each other. A similar policy applies to obedience classes. What may not be so well known is that about two-thirds of all of the all-breed judging panels submitted to AKC cannot be initially approved because of a conflict on the part of one or more of the proposed judges. Not the least of the problem is the difficulty many judges encounter in determining whether or not a show is under or over 200 miles from a similar event to which they are committed. On whose map is the 200 miles measured? What constitutes 30 days from a given date in a month containing 28 or 29 days or 31 days. What is 30 days from today, for example?

In studying this policy, it also becomes apparent that it was designed for dog show realities in the Northeast such as they were perhaps 40 years ago. Then, as now, the densely populated Northeast had many shows within a small geographic range in comparison to other parts of the country. It is clear that the 200 mile restriction is not equally valid in all areas of the country.

In conducting its review, your Board had three fundamental concerns. First, it was essential to protect the right of exhibitors to have a chance to show their dogs under a wide variety of judges in their general area. Second, it was important that any change in policy not unreasonably diminish the number of assignments a judge can realistically expect to judge in the course of a year. Third, any change in policy must not make it more difficult for a club to put a judging panel together.

It is also clear that any new policy must be easily understood and, therefore, easily administered by clubs and judges alike.

As you will see from the map which will be published as part of the minutes of this meeting (page 168) and which you will shortly be receiving, the Continental United States has been divided into eight zones. Each zone has a roughly equal number of all-breed shows in it. Since the number of all-breed shows is roughly equal for each of the eight zones, it is possible to set one limit on the number of assignments a judge can accept in any zone. This means that a particular judge can only judge a fixed percentage of any competition in a zone over a calendar year.

Specifically, within each zone, a judge may judge the same competition, be it a breed, a group, a regular obedience class or Best in Show, twice from January 1 to June 30 and twice from July 1 to December 31. There will be no required time lapse between any two assignments, except that no judge will be approved to judge two assignments, for the same competition in any one zone or in any contiguous zones if the assignments in question are at companion shows (two or three shows on a weekend, for example), or at shows that are part of a "circuit."

It might appear that this policy is more liberal than 200-mile-30-day policy, but this is not true. Under the 200-mile-30-day policy, a judge can theoretically judge the same breed once every 30 days or 12 times a year in a given area. The new policy would permit this same judge to judge a given breed a total of only four times. Your Board believes the new policy accomplishes its primary objective of insuring that exhibitors will have a wide variety of judges to choose from over the year in their general area. In addition, it does not reduce the number of assignments a judge could reasonably expect to judge during the year, nor does it increase the difficulty clubs would encounter in compiling a judging panel.

A survey of many judges' judging records show that if the new policy had been in effect in 1978, these judges would have been able to judge virtually every assignment they actually did judge that year. In other words, judges will be able to judge with approximately the same frequency under the new policy as under the old, Since actual judging assignments will not be appreciably changed, it is fair to say that clubs will not experience any more difficulty in compiling their panels.

Under the new policy, however, judges will no longer be required to be mileage experts. Mileage and date computations will not be neces-

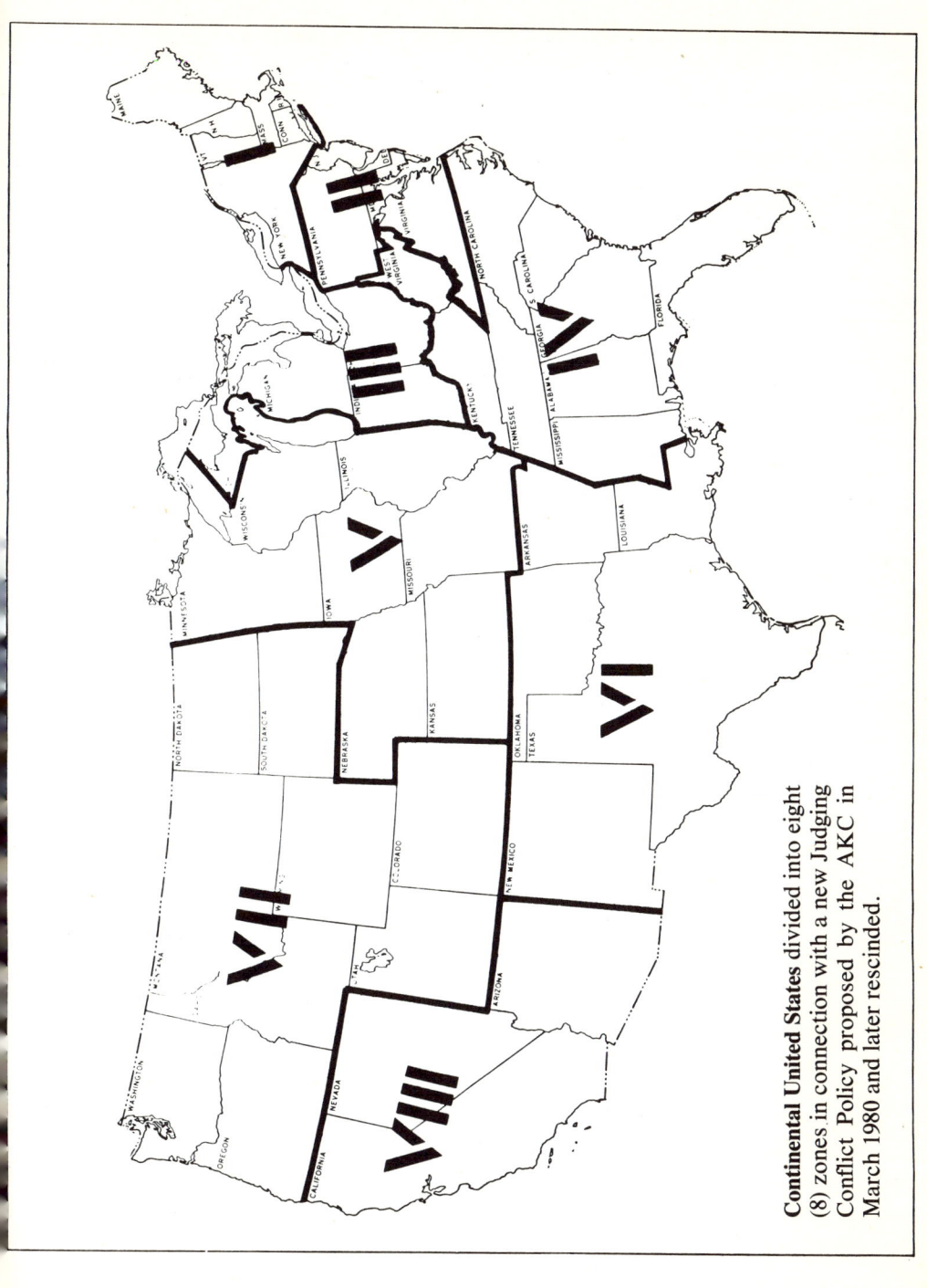

Continental United States divided into eight (8) zones in connection with a new Judging Conflict Policy proposed by the AKC in March 1980 and later rescinded.

sary. A judge simply needs to look at a map and can know at a glance whether any two shows are in the same zone, and therefore, potentially in conflict. Thus, the number of conflicts will diminish, which, of course, will be good news to any Show Chairman who has been faced with the unpleasant task of salvaging a judging panel ravaged by conflicts.

As I have said, the new policy will become effective January 1, 1981. Enforcement during the first year will be reasonably liberal, so that commitments already made by clubs and judges are not adversely affected. Please examine the map and my comments on the policy which you will receive as part of the minutes of this meeting. Any comments or observations will be greatly appreciated.

If you have any questions about possible conflicts call the Show Plans Department of the American Kennel Club and ask for a ruling.

It is important to keep in mind not only the AKC's policy governing time and distance between given shows, but also that some clubs have restrictions of their own above and beyond those of the AKC. Many larger shows and specialty events fall into this category. Their restrictions become part of the contractual agreement between the judge and the club and should be clearly stipulated with specific time span or state lines in the confirming letter which acts as a binding contract.

Besides the above restrictions, you also have to consider whether or not you have the time and facilities to get from one show to another within the schedule allotted. In this jet age it is possible to officiate in California on Saturday and New York on Sunday provided you have the stamina to withstand jet-lag and airport hassles. But what is the actual method employed by the AKC in granting permission for such high-flying meanderings?

The rule of thumb is that a judge has to be able to prove he has the capability of leaving the Saturday show at a reasonable time, getting to the departing airport and being able to fly out on several flights, arriving at the destination with sufficient time to permit rest before the Sunday show. To allow for unforeseen circumstances, several airlines must be flying to the same airport with many back-up flights available. Since judges are not supposed to request early group order or breed judging to speed up their departure from one show in order to catch a flight for the next show, the computations needed to determine whether they can make it in time would make even Einstein dizzy.

The previous paragraphs have dealt with the subject of external restrictions. What about internal restraints or individual limitations that judges may impose on themselves—do they exist? Most definitely, yes.

82

Some of these restraints are brought about through physical necessity, such as ability only to judge a figure less than the 175 maximum number of dogs a day, a desire for only one show a weekend, nothing indoors, shows within a specified distance from home and so on.

Sometimes judges will not accept assignments that would interfere with their family vacation plans, special occasions, the desire to take a month or so off during the summer or extra days in the midst of holiday periods.

There are also personal, well thought-out reasons for establishing certain limitations. It is not unusual for conscientious judges to carefully assess their longterm judging goals and make their plans accordingly. These adjudicators are aware of their responsibilities to the clubs and exhibitors. They do not want to wear out their welcome in a given area by officiating too often over the same breed or breeds. Therefore, they will turn down assignments when they feel such a likelihood would exist.

It is easy to understand that accepting assignments is not merely a matter of looking on one's calendar and locating a free date. Instead, multi-faceted considerations must be undertaken before the final word can be determined. The judge who plans ahead and keeps concise records is prepared to render his decisions quickly without much ado.

Calendars

Trying to keep a calendar of assignments which is easy to decipher at a quick glance is problem for most judges. You need not only to correlate all shows according to status (inquiry or confirmed), but also dates, locations, actual assignments and travel time. All this has little to say about additional room needed for normal family activities that preclude you from being available on given days.

The problems you encounter in keeping a calendar depends on the amount of judging you do during a year. If you officiate two or three times a year (which most judges do), you can easily use the family wall calendar to write in your show information and still leave room for junior's baseball games, golf matches, bridge parties and family holidays.

Judges who are busy most weekends need to establish a calendar that is specifically suited for their requirements. One example of such a calendar, which can be purchased in many stationery stores, features large squares for each day of the year and comes segmented into months. Hanging on the wall near the telephone, this calendar will provide enough room for a judge to write down pertinent information regarding his shows and enables him to tell at a glance just where he stands in relation to conflicts. Being able to see an entire month at once and having to flip only monthly pages forward and backward for the prior month makes it easier to determine what restrictions, if any, exist.

If you cannot stand the idea of a hanging calendar, perhaps a weekly diary would suffice. The desk diary, which could be kept near the phone with all assignments placed in their proper dates, is easy to use but its one drawback is the fact that you cannot visualize a monthly picture and must turn several pages to assess possible conflicts.

Since you are dealing with both unconfirmed telephone and personal contact inquiries and written confirmation assignments, it is necessary to show the difference on your calendar. The easiest method is to mark your assignments with different colored pens and pencil.

All unconfirmed assignments should be entered in pencil, giving the name of the show, location and breeds requested. Once the assignments are confirmed, the pencil markings can be erased and blue ink notations made denoting a contractual agreement. If you have a confirmed show date, but not definite assignment, use a different color pen as identification of this variance. When the breeds, group and/or best in show are known, write over with blue ink. Now you can quickly tell just what the status is of each show entered on your calendar.

If an assignment comes in that is for a future year not listed in your calendar or desk diary, write the pertinent information in the back, listing shows in chronological order and transfer the data to the new year's calendar as soon as it is available for purchase.

Filing System

In case you thought you had already accomplished enough secretarial work for one show, don't relax because it isn't over yet. You still have to maintain adequate files for not only that show, but all other shows as well.

A filing system enables you to have all your judging correspondence in one place instead of stuffing it in the checkbook, with paid bills, or in between pages of a cookbook or the latest best-selling novel. In short, everything that has to do with your judging career needs to be kept together in a designated file cabinet or drawer.

If you officiate at only a couple of shows a year, your filing system will not be too entailed. You really only need two letter-size manila folders: one for current shows and the other for past events. Inside the folders keep all original correspondence you received from the club, as well as copies of letters you sent to them. The shows need to be segregated and all data for each show stapled together. Your folder for current or future shows should be labeled as such and the shows inside need to be listed on the outside of the folder in chronological order by date with the name of the kennel club and specific assignment. By writing this information outside the folder, you can immediately tell where you stand and what facts you should find inside the file. Once the show date has passed, take the data out pertaining to that particular show and place it in the "past shows" folder. Cross off reference to the show that appears on the outside of the current file.

Multi-group and all-breed judges need to have a more involved system. Instead of having only one folder, they need separate folders for each year as their shows may run at least three years into the future. Again, all data detailing a particular show needs to be stapled together and cross-referenced as to contents written on the outside of each file. Time span covered therein should be written on the folder's label.

Shows that are still in the query stage need to be so designated on the outside of the files. Use a system that corresponds with the one you use on your calendars: pencil for initial inquiries, blue ink for full confirmed assignments and red ink for definite shows but unknown breeds. Expiration dates need to be noted in pencil opposite those shows where a definite time period was given for final confirmation. Once a date has passed and you have not received your contractual agreement, you are free to accept other shows.

5

Preparing for
the Show

Image

HAVE YOU EVER GIVEN MUCH THOUGHT to just what it is that sets certain judges apart from the others? Or why you respect a particular judge more than his cohorts even though you do not necessarily always agree with his selections? Or even why some judges look as if they know what they are doing when, it actuality, they may not?

Image is the key word here; to be more specific: the appearance of authority, stature, competence, confidence and knowledge. You need to act the part, look the part and be the part to convey the successful image.

The aura one transmits in the ring must not be affected; judges should *not* strut around the ring like peacocks and award winnings with grandiose effervescence. A superior, know-it-all attitude repels exhibitors, handlers and those at ringside. An arrogant, assertive adjudicator cannot command respect. Rather he makes his friends and enemies regard him with distaste and repulsion.

On the other hand, the timid, unassuming judge will not command respect. A weak person who has little self-confidence in himself or his judgments cannot expect others to have much faith in his decisions. The meek judge is easily swayed, flounders back and forth and operates in total confusion. This type of person often bends over backward to show favoritism to friends, can be controlled by big-name handlers and oscillates in trying to come to any kind of decision at all. He quickly loses whatever self-esteem he may have had as he distrusts his own judgment, intelligence and ability.

The judge who performs with friendliness and jocularity, trying to please everyone, in reality pleases no one. Those who seem to be laughing with him may be laughing at him.

A good adjudicator has to walk a fine line and it is very easy to fall into easy traps. Two illustrations of pitfalls follow:

The brand-new judge, having passed his provisional and received full status, is very often so proud of his illusive success that he unconsciously transmits this feeling when he steps into the ring as a fully ranked arbitrator. So impressed is he by the power which has been granted to him to make or break kings, find new stars and render his own judgment that he rides on a massive ego trip. In subsequent years, as he has more opportunities to practice his trade, he will become more self-assured, settling into his position with greater ease as he personally comes to terms with his responsibilities and decisions. In most cases (unfortunately not all), ego-trips gradually slide away, leaving in their wake truly dedicated judges.

On the opposite side of the line exists a judge who is having psychological problems in accepting the burdens of his decisions. He lacks self-esteem and is weakened by his desire to be well-thought of by all. He begins to become increasingly concerned over the fact that his initial high entries are not sustained, even though it is a well-known fact that once exhibitors have had the opportunity to assess the type of dog preferred, thereby categorizing the judge, entries will fall off. This anxious judge who places more emphasis on the number of dogs entered under him will do anything to protect those numbers. He begins to function indiscriminately, handing out wins to spread the wealth around. Exhibitors will enter under him, not because they value his opinion, but rather they know that anything goes. This judge may be able to say to himself, "Look at those entries. I'm really a great judge!" In actuality, however, a win under this particular type of person is neither sought after nor covertly prized.

Therefore it behooves all judges to be aware of the image they are projecting as this is the mirror in which others see them. A judge needs to be assertive without being pushy, self-confident without being cocky, and maintain self-esteem without arrogance. Most important of all, he must be candid with himself and engage in honest self-critism. In doing so, he will be able to truly recognize his faults, take the steps to correct them and in turn, project the proper image of a successful, well-thought-of adjudicator.

What to Wear

You certainly cannot judge a book by its cover, nor can you determine the inner makings of a person by the clothes he wears. Nevertheless, it is true that appearances count a great deal in our society. Appearance is comprised not only of personality and body language, but also of the clothing that envelopes the whole package. So clothing must be a prime consideration of every judge who wants to project the appropriate image of authority.

The clothes you wear must not only suit the particular type of show or social function, but must also fit properly, wear well and be totally comfortable. Clothing should be a source of pleasure. What you wear should make you feel good, allow you to enjoy yourself more and permit you to function as a respected arbiter. Being comfortable and properly attired do not always run parallel with each other, making your task in selecting the right outfits arduous and time-consuming. However, if you persevere in choosing clothes that cannot be dated, are free of restraints and casual in appearance, you will soon accumulate a wardrobe that fits any ocassion.

When selecting clothes, take a good look at yourself in the mirror—is the dress or pants too tight, seams straight and/or smooth, the pattern overpowering? Do you have enough freedom to bend over from the shoulders and down from the knees? Do you appear as if you are going to a baseball game instead of judging a dog show? The latter is more important than many people realize. Yes, dog shows are a sport and therefore call for casual attire. But the position of an officiator carries more weight than a participant. You need to look as if you belong in the center of the ring.

In deciding what to pack or wear to a show, you should keep in mind the type and ambience of the event. If the show is indoors, what is the flooring? Will there be sufficient heat or is the armory cold and drafty? On the other hand, will there be air-conditioning if the time of year and location of show warrant its use? Outdoor shows have particular problems of their own, namely weather and grounds. You need to be prepared for just about any kind of weather and this is not always easy when you can only fit so much clothing into a flight bag. If you have any questions at all about what you need for a particular show, ask the show chairman or hospitality person for their advice. They are the ones who are most familiar with their event and know approximately what you can expect.

Guidelines for Men

The image you want to project in your attire as a judge is certainly not the same as if you were merely one of the boys in the field. Your clothes need to give off an aura of authority, not camaraderie. The passé, cheesy leisure-suit is out. Instead you should wear business suits or well-coordinated sports jacket and slacks, such as a navy blue blazer with grey slacks. Dark colors in either solid, pinstripes or understated plaids look terrific. Anything too boisterous, light or overpowering should be avoided. The fit of the jacket and pants should allow enough room for you to kneel and bend over. Some judges recommend selecting something a size larger, while others say a good tailor can make the necessary adjustments.

Shirts and ties can be varied to give the impression of an entirely new outfit each time you judge. Shirts that are either white, medium or light blue, beige or pale yellow seem to work well. Ties and bowties are a mixed bag running from striped, ivy league, club, small polka-dot, plaid, paisley, to solid. Socks and shoes should be dark and simple, unless you feel so conservatively dressed that you like to make a statement of your own by wearing bright red socks that would show every time you kneel down to examine a dog. Otherwise, your total outfit should be color coordinated to blend in well and not overstate the effect.

Frequently, some men have difficulties in selecting the right individual items that combine in making the over-all look. They either neglect to visualize the entire package or do not have the eye to see items together. If you fall in this bracket, go shopping with a friend whose taste you admire and ask him or her to help you. Very often persons who are always well-dressed have a natural sense of taste—a feeling of what styles, colors, fabrics and lines blend together. They are also aware of figure problems and know how to avoid traps.

Guidelines for Women

The fashion emphasis is placed more solidly on the woman's shoulders than on her male counterpart. This decrees the variety of colors, fabrics and styles existing in feminine apparel. But the larger selection is not always appropriate as most of the clothes for women appearing on the racks are dictated by current fashion trends which frequently place a greater accent on sales than on wearability or pleasing appearance.

Women also have another issue to consider and that is how to give off the semblance of authority without losing their femininity. Although women's lib has made inroads, this is still a man's world and dog shows are no different. Before a hue and cry arises, it is necessary to realize that even though women are more active in breeding and showing and are about equal in numbers as breed judges, men, by and large, have the superior stance of belonging and being in power where it counts. It is still easier for both men and women to accept a man's judgment over that of a woman, unless that female has arrived and gained a position of respect and honor through years of hard work. There are only a few of these around and to the rest lie the responsibility of trying to hold their own.

To achieve the necessary stature, you cannot dress in frilly, strictly feminine clothing for judging. Pastels are out and decisive colors are in; fashion trends are out and classics are in; flowery prints or loud strips and patterns should be kept for the house as simplicity must reign in the ring.

Basically, you would be best advised to purchase only clothing that shows you to your advantage, while being able to communicate to all that you have the knowledge and ability to function as a respected judge. Suits with accompanying simple blouses and dresses with matching jackets seem to fit this to a ''t,'' provided they are tailored and well-fitted. Anything with a straight skirt should be avoided as you would not have enough freedom to kneel comfortably. Slits up the side, back or front may permit the necessary movement but lead an observer to concentrate more on the legs and less on whatever mental assets you may possess. See-through garments should be avoided for the same reason.

Whether or not women should wear pantsuits for judging is a subject that leads to a variety of opinions. It cannot be denied that a majority of the women in this country are more comfortable in pants than in a skirt or dress. There is an ease in freedom of movement when one wears pants.

All too frequently the type of pantsuits one sees at dog shows are ill-fitting, cheaply made and of the wrong color or pattern. Often these outfits are worn by women who have neither the figure nor grace to enhance the suit. If you can wear one, then by all means purchase a good quality, well-fitted, simply styled outfit and keep it in your closet for those miserable, wet, cold, windy shows where everyone is chilled to the bone. On days such as this your main thought should be in wearing something that not only looks appropriate and good on you, but is also warm enough to enable you to function without too much hindrance from the cold.

The shoes you wear for judging should be sensible and comfortable. Extremely high heels are an impossibility. For indoor—wear something with rubber soles will help to cushion your feet and prevent slipping.

The Weather

In adverse weather conditions many believe clothing styles should go out the window. This does not have to be the case if you are prepared to meet whatever comes head on. For those blistery, hot days, men and women should be attired in clothing that allows their bodies to breathe. Suits, shirts and dresses should be purchased with this in mind. Polyester is a known inhibitor and pity the poor judge who stands out in the hot sun all day in an outfit comprised chiefly of this material. Cotton/poly blends are an improvement and natural blends are the best of all, provided the item has been treated with a wrinkle-free substance. In extreme heat a man may wish to remove his jacket, but not his tie, for judging during the day. For group or best in show officiating, put the jacket back on no matter how hot it may be. The principal purpose for doing this is that group and best in show judging is a different process with different meaning than breed judging and should be treated as such. Hats, but not those belonging on a sailboat, should be worn by those who are sensitive to the sun and sunblock cream needs to be regularly applied to exposed skin areas.

On the days when the heavens open and rain comes pouring down by the bucketfull while the tents are about to be carried away in the wind, the judge is constantly exposed to the elements. Regardless of his own personal discomfiture, he still has to carry on with proper judicial bearing and try to determine which animal muds the best. If you have proper rain gear, which you have remembered to pack, you are in good shape to survive the elements. The two-piece rain suit that one visualizes as being worn by an old sea captain on a galeswept schooner off the coast of Maine is perfect for a dog show. With insulated rubber boots, coordinated in color with the rain suit, you are ready to take charge. Women who may regard these outfits with horror, can keep dry and warm with quality fashionable waterproof raincoats and high boots. Hair can be kept neat and tidy beneath a rain hat or water resistant scarf.

A cold, sunless day when the windchill factor goes into the depths and unheated buildings in the fall, winter and early spring present other problems. A judge who is chilled to the bone will hardly be able to move about, much less be in any frame of mind to render justifiable decisions. He is quite likely to award first prize to the first dog he sees in his quest to complete his assignment and retreat to heated quarters. Thermal underwear has made astonishing gains from the early days of bulkiness and discomfiture. Lightweight thermal attire which comes in a variety of colors and patterns will do much to help keep you warm. Insulated, lined boots can keep the toes from freezing and specially designed stockings will keep the legs from turning blue. Layers of clothing are best, so bundle up in jackets, vests or sweaters. Bulky coats that inhibit movement should be avoided.

The biggest problem to overcome is frozen fingers. You cannot wear gloves while judging and hands cannot be continuously thrust in the pockets. Pocketwarmers, which are small heating elements used by skiers, are a possibility to consider.

Accessories

Jewelry needs to be kept to a minmum. Not only because too much silver or gold is ostentatious, but it also detracts from the individual. Large pieces that clang and clank or ring and chime should not be worn. And the same holds true for big breast baubles that dangle on a chain and can end up in some dog's face when you lean over to examine him. When contemplating what pieces of jewelry to wear, remember that quality and not quantity should be your first guide.

Watches are needed by all judges. You need to keep track of your judging time and mark it in the judge's book, know when you are due in the ring, how much time you have for lunch, and so on. Conventional dials are frequently used, as are the digital watches that give the time down to the second with just a push of a small button. Caution must be observed when using certain types of digitals at outdoor shows as sometimes there is difficulty in reading the figures in bright sunlight.

Corsages and boutonnieres may be appropriate for a prom, but have definite drawbacks in the dog show ring. The main problem lies with the fact that some dogs think the flowers are something good to eat, while others may regard the petals as enemies to be avoided at all costs.

Regions

What you wear to judge at shows in the section of the country you live in may not be appropriate at shows in another area. For example, in the northeast, which is known for traditionalism and conservatism, the country-boy, down-on-the-farm look would be hideously out of place. Similarily the staid, navy-suited, white shirt ivy league appearance could give an impression of stiffness at certain shows in the mid-west or south. It is necessary to avoid looking "too formal, too drab or too much," but you must also refrain from appearing as if you are at a picnic, going to the movies or on a hayride.

Not only do you have to take under consideration the region in which you are judging, but also the type of show: indoors or out, formal or informal, large or small. The only clue that could assist you in trying to determine the ambience of a particular kennel club is past performances, either from personal knowledge or hearsay. Generally speaking, the larger shows or those with point restrictions are run on a more formal basis than the small shows with under 1000 dogs held on some county fairgrounds.

Deciding what to wear, when to wear it and how it should be worn is taxing on the nerves and the budget. However, if you purchase and wear clothing with all these data in mind, you will have accumulated a wardrobe that will suffice in any region of the country at any type of show.

Remember that classics as opposed to fads adhere forever. An item that fits well, is properly made and pleasant to look at will be around for as long as you are, provided your figure does not undergo any drastic changes. Your clothes should never be permitted to outshine you, but rather be a part of the over-all package of authority and responsibility you want to present as a judge.

What to Take

Judging requires a great deal of traveling, and regardless of whether you are scurrying around airports, or loading and unloading your car, you either take too much stuff or not enough. Usually the item you forgot and left at home hanging in the closet is just the one you need the most. Many judges have a master list of things they need to pack which they keep either in a drawer or permanently in a suitcase. Include on your list not only all clothing and accessories required for judging or social functions, but also all club information, schedule, tickets and correspondence. This material should be kept with you at all times.

Two items in particular you should consider taking along are an alarm clock and a portable radio. The alarm clock should be included because, even though you may make a call to the front desk for a specific wake-up time, the personnel on duty have been known to lose that request. Many judges have had to scurry around in the morning without breakfast, just barely getting to the show in time because wake-up calls were missed. The alarm clock, when set for five to ten minutes after wake-up time, can serve as a back-up system. A small portable radio permits you to not only have music of your own selection, instead of the current disco music that many motels favor, but also keeps you apprised of latest weather forecasts.

What kind of suitcase you prefer to use depends on how you are traveling, the amount of items you plan on taking and your length of time on the road. If you are driving your problems are minor as you can load everything you possibly need in the automobile with plenty of room to spare. Dresses or suits, enclosed in appropriate hanging bags, can be hung on the clothing hook inside the car or laid down flat on the back seat. Other items can be packed in a small overnight bag. Raingear or cold-weather coats and boots can be automatically included without concern for space.

Traveling by plane is a different matter altogether. Not only must you be aware of the space limitations in one bag, but you need to be sure you do not load it with so much stuff that it is too heavy for you to carry around acres of airports. Generally there are two types of bags that are ideal for airplanes: the hanging/folding garment bag and the small under-the-seater. You may want to use one or both depending on the duration of your stay away from home. The advantage of the hanging bag is that you can hang the bag in a closet on the airplane and your clothes will not be quite as wrinkled as they would be if folded. A small suitcase which can fit under the seat will be sufficient for most overnight runs. Bags made of waterproof and stainproof fabrics are not as heavy as those of solid construction, but if good quality, are just as durable.

Packing Tips

1) Always carry with you all vital medical information regarding chronic ailments or disabilities. Place in your wallet a list containing blood type, prescription medication currently used and name, address and telephone number of your doctor.

2) Wear a Medic Alert bracelet if you need one.

3) If you wear glasses and need them desperately to see, travel with an extra pair.

4) Sunglasses are great for blocking both the sun's brilliant rays and the particle laden city air, but should not be worn while judging.

5) Purchase suitcases or hanging bags that are not only well constructed, but lightweight. It is amazing how even fabric bags become heavier and heavier as you tote them on and off planes, and around miles of airport corridors.

6) Place ladies' shoes heel to toe in fabric shoemits and pack them on the bottom of the bag. If you are taking two pairs, place them on opposite sides to evenly distribute the weight.

7) Men's shoes should also be enclosed in shoemits and placed on opposite sides. If you are using a softsided bag, put breakable items, such as alarm clock, inside the shoes.

8) Intermingle clothing within the suitcase. Trousers should be carefully folded on the creaselines and put in the bag top to bottom and bottom to top. Suit jackets should be buttoned and hung on the hanger face down, with the collar next to the hinge. Pull the sleeves back and smooth the arms. Bring the trousers up over the jacket

and then fold the bottom of the jacket carefully over the pants.

9) Cardboard holders should be removed from men's shirts. Socks can be rolled up and put inside the collars to hold them in shape. Shirts should be buttoned and folded from the sleeve line down and then the bottom brought up from the back.

10) Underwear can be rolled together and stuffed in vacant corners of the bag to keep items from shifting around.

11) For hanging bags, put as much together as you can. Jackets, trousers and shirts can be hung together. Button the shirts but not the jackets. Instead fold the lapels over and smooth the item before hanging another article or zipping the bag.

12) Ladies' dresses should be first folded in thirds vertically along the bust and leg lines before being placed in a conventional bag. They should be packed lengthwise, alternating the collars from right to left. The skirt portion should be left outside the bag until all the dresses are packed and then folded in over each other.

13) Ladies' suits can be packed in a similar fashion as men's with the difference being that the skirts should be folded vertically into thirds before being placed in the bag and all lines smoothed out as much as possible.

14) Lingerie should be coordinated and placed in plastic bags according to sets. Stockings may be stuffed in corners.

15) Folding garment bags are great for keeping wrinkles out if those items most likely to wrinkle are hung on the outside and those most likely to stay wrinkle-free hung on the inside. Then when the bag is folded over, the articles that will be pinched the most will show the least effects.

16) All breakable items should be cushioned between layers of clothing and packed according to where the weight distribution is least apt to be felt.

17) Include extra plastic bags for soiled articles.

18) In spite of careful packing, some items will be wrinkled. If this is the case, hang the garment on the towel rack in the bathroom and run the tub water at full force, maximum heat, to steam the wrinkles out.

19) Or place the garment flat down on the bed, smooth out the wrinkles with your hand which has been dampened with tap water. Place the item over the back of a chair with the heaviest end hanging down, putting pressure on the rest of the garment.

20) Try to use only lightweight containers. For example, jewelry cases should be made of fabric rather than heavier construction.

21) Transfer cosmetics and the like to small plastic containers and refill when necessary. When refilling, squeeze air from the bottles and recap tightly before packing to allow for air expansion at jet altitudes.

22) Instead of buying special containers, make an initial purchase of items in small quantities and refill the bottles.

23) Buy nail remover pads, instead of bottled remover that may evaporate while in flight.

24) Paper towels should be placed on the bottom of a man's grooming kit to absorb any moisture that accumulates.

25) Pack a long-handled bristle brush in a plastic bag for brisk rubdowns in the shower or bath after or before a day's work in the ring.

26) If you have dentures, be sure to take along a repair kit for temporary emergency repairs.

27) Scotch tape is a good item to take with you for quick patching-ups.

28) A clothes brush will remove any dog hair or accumulated dust and dirt after a day's judging.

29) If you like a special nip before bedtime, pack a small plastic bottle of your favorite liquid refreshment.

30) Above all, before you leave home, coordinate your wardrobe and accessories. If you travel a lot, keep a bag packed at all times with necessary grooming items, so that all you have to do is to put in and remove clothing before and after each weekend.

6

Traveling Tips

A GOOD TRAVEL AGENT can be a judge's best friend. Once your agent is trained to understand some of the particularities that surround your travel arrangements—such as trying to make seemingly impossible connections, getting you out to the boondocks with the most efficient mode of transportation and suffering with you as you endeavor to get back home Sunday evening at a reasonable hour for work the next morning—you can sit back and leave all the planning to him. Just apprise him of your schedule and let him figure out how you can meet all your requirements.

Judges who do a lot of traveling spend more time in the airports than in the sky. Every effort should be made to cut that wasted time to a minimum, yet allow ample opportunity to make all necessary transfers. An agent has the data at hand to advise you if you can make that thirty minute connection given the size of the airport, known delays, location of the airlines and whether or not you check your bags. Try to always procure a copy of the layout of any large airport in which you have to scurry about transferring on different airlines. Have at hand your line, flight number and destination, as well as enough other information to provide you with backup flights in case a connection is missed. Your agent can provide you with this material.

A travel agent is also the best person to advise you if you are eligible for any of the special fares that are available. Regulations and constant changes make interpretation for the layman difficult at best. Also, if you are a steady customer, your agent may bill you for total costs and permit payment upon your return from the weekend shows. This is a big advantage as you will not have to juggle your bank accounts, nor overload credit cards. Since you are paid at the show, it is relatively simple for you to deposit the club's check upon returning home, and issue a check to your travel agent at the same time. This makes your bookkeeping simpler to manage.

If you decide to rent a car, the agent can take care of all administrative details and your car will be waiting for you at your destination airport.

The use of a travel agent does not cost you any money directly out of your own pocket, as he is paid by the companies he serves and you would be remiss in not taking advantage of his services. So, locate a good travel agent, trust him and use his specialities to the upmost. You will find your traveling to be much easier.

SPECIAL SERVICES

Official Airline Guide

If you are a frequent flyer, who always wants to know just where you are going, with alternate flights and schedules to permit changes, you should consider subscribing to the *Official Airline Guide*. The North American Edition is the one most of our judges would need. It shows direct and connecting flights and fares of all scheduled airlines in the United States, Mexico, Canada and the Caribbean, departure and arrival times, types of aircraft, meal service and stops en route. A year's subscription for the handy pocket guide is $62.00 for twelve monthly issues. For further information, contact the publishers: Reuben H. Donnelley Corporation, 2000 Clearwater Drive, Oak Brook, Illinois 50521.

Airline Passengers Association

The APA is an organization formed for the principal purpose of providing assistance to passengers who frequently use the airlines. The Association works as an effective lobby in Washington and with airlines to bring about better service. It publishes a travel magazine, as well as newsletters designed to keep consumers current with airline functions, advice and warnings on travel arrangement and helpful hints. The APA also acts as a traveler's insurance group which provides extensive coverage with a variety of rates to suit an individual's needs. Many judges who belong to this organization have been known to flash their membership cards whenever they have encountered particular problems and believe that their difficulties were handled quicker than if they had not apprised the airline personnel that they were members. Dues are based on the amount of insurance coverage requested. For additional information, write to the Airline Passengers' Association, P.O. Box 2758, Dallas, Texas 75221.

Airline Clubs

One particular benefit for travelers that was originally established gratis for businessmen who logged x number of miles with a specific airline but which has now been opened for a fee to the general traveler, is the Club organizations sponsored by most of the major airlines. Membership fees range from $25.00 to $35.00 a year, with reduced rate for three-year prepayments or lifetime. There are many advantages to belonging to a Club if you frequently travel on one airline that has such a service in your home airport. There are club rooms that feature peace and privacy, while being easily accessible to gates; seating arrangements are comfortable with ready access to telephones, color TV or stereo and liquid refreshments; a receptionist is on hand to help with last minute reservations and to grant priority changes, seat selections and hand out boarding passes. The club membership also affords check cashing privileges and special baggage tags which signal status to airport and inflight personnel.

From the tired judge's point of view, it is unfortunate that the facilities are not open twenty-four hours a day and are not available in all airports. Usually, the club rooms are only established in the carrier's major airports and open during the heavy traveled times from seven in the morning to eight or nine at night.

WHAT TO DO WHEN THINGS GO WRONG

Lost Bags

We have all heard stories of judges who arrived at their destination only to find that their bags went someplace else. If this should happen to you, what steps should you take?

First, determine that the bag is really lost and not just sitting in a dark corner. Ask the baggage handler to search thoroughly among other luggage for yours. If it is not there, go at once to the supervisor. Fill out the "Notice of Baggage Irregularity" claim form, which asks you for physical description of the bag, contents, estimated value, departure and arrival details, where the bag can be delivered if found and so forth. Do not surrender your claim ticket but insist that a copy be made for the airline while you keep the original.

Even if the airline personnel insist that your bag is only temporarily delayed, treat the delay as a loss and do not depend on receiving your luggage before you get back home, if ever. Therefore, be sure you have the name of the people you have spoken with and copies of all claimant forms you have filled out and signed.

It is a little advertised fact that airlines are required to compensate you for any inconvenience and will pay up to $750.00 for emergency supplies for domestic losses. After filing the necessary forms, go immediately to the airline ticket counter and request money to replace those items you will need while you are away from home. Every airline honors one of these three procedures: cash, chits for use at airport shops or reimbursement at later date upon presentation of receipts. Check first before you act and be sure to get something in writing to substantiate any further claim you may have to make. Even if your baggage has been tracked down and will be delayed overnight, you are still entitled to replacements for clothing and toiletries, especially if you have not only a judge's dinner to attend that evening but also the show the next day. It is conceivable that the airline would not be able to return your bag to you in time for a 7:30 a.m. motel departure for the show grounds.

Airlines are not known to volunteer this compensation, so be sure to let them know you are aware of the statute and your legal rights. If the airline has not been able to trace your baggage, file a detailed claim form within forty-five days and keep on top of the matter until you receive just compensation.

Damaged Bags

Any damage to your luggage that occurred en route is subject to monetary reimbursement. As with lost bags, damaged items on domestic flights are covered up to a limit of $750.00. If you notice that your bag is damaged when you pick it up at the baggage claim area, go at once to the airline ticket counter and fill out the preliminary "Baggage Damage Report." Keep a copy of the report for your files and be sure to write down the name of the airline personnel who assisted you in your claim. Let them see the damage so that they are ready to attest to the fact that your baggage was marred. Once again, be sure to file the final official claimant form, which will be sent to you by the airline, within forty-five days for domestic flights, seven days for international flights.

Bumping

As judges are usually running to and fro, from airport to airport, line to line, with little time to spare, they can be likely targets for bumping if an airline has overbooked a particular flight. Therefore, it behooves all judges to acquaint themselves with current regulations regarding overbooking and know just what to do if they are confronted with a bumping situation.

Every carrier has its own policies regarding who should and should not be denied boarding, but most adopt the theory that late check-ins, late arrivals at boarding gates and passengers who paid discounted fares are those persons most apt to require a different flight if the one for which they had a reservation has filled beyond its capacity. Usually the airline will first ask for volunteers who are willing to give up their seats in exchange for monetary payment that generally is equivalent to the price of the ticket. Not enough volunteers will result in involuntary denied boarding for persons in the categories listed above.

If you are denied a seat, keep cool and rational. Request the following assistance:

a) Next flight to get you at your destination within two hours (domestic) and four hours (international) of your previous scheduled arrival time;

b) If a different carrier is needed to meet this requirement, be sure to have this avenue confirmed;

c) Arrange for immediate compensation equal to your ticket price or not less than $37.50 nor more than $200.00;

d) If a flight cannot be found which will get you at your destination within the allotted timespan, you are entitled to additional compensation, so procure this amount as well.

e) If you are unable to make a connecting flight, let the airline know that you are entitled to compensation for this missed flight;

f) Be aware that you do not have to accept alternate flights to different airports within the same metropolitan area;

g) Call the show chairman or hospitality chairman, or whoever is supposed to meet you and advise them of your difficulties.

Delayed or Cancelled Flights

Most judges have stories to tell of sitting in an airport or on a plane for hours waiting for mechanical or weather problems to clear. Once again, this is an area where you need to know exactly what to do because most airline personnel are not willing to volunteer the information:

a) If mechanical troubles arise, try to get a concise idea of just what the problem is, how long it will take to fix it and what your alternatives are;

b) If weather related, look for alternate means of transportation to get you where you want to go, i.e. renting a car or public transportation;

c) Let the airline know that you have a set schedule that must be adhered to if at all possible and ask for assistance;

d) If you are delayed for more than four hours, you are entitled to meals and access to telephone or telegraph facilities, as well as limited ground transportation;

e) Hotel/motel accommodations are provided if your delay occurs between the hours of ten p.m. and six a.m.;

f) Meals are provided if you would have received the same on the delayed flight. Get a chit for the same from the airline personnel;

g) Cancelled flights require the same assistance to its passengers as those temporarily delayed. Do not be afraid to ask for any help you need;

h) Be sure, if the flight is cancelled, that you are on the very next plane leaving for your destination, regardless if a different airline is involved;

i) All airlines have different variations of any of the above. Ask questions to find out the exact services and assistance to which you are entitled;

j) If you are being met at you destination airport, let the meeting party know of any delays or changed plans. If you will not be able to get to the show in time, also let them know as soon as possible;

k) Last but not least, don't give up. If you persevere, yet are courteous while doing so, most airlines will move mountains to get you where you want to go as quickly as they can.

Flying Tips

1) If at all practicable, carry your bag on board and stow it in the baggage compartment adjacent to your seat, or in the hanging closets.

2) Always have on hand the name and telephone number of the show chairman, hospitality chairman and/or judges' committee chairman.

3) Keep with you all dog show information, standards and correspondence.

4) Likewise, items of value, such as jewelry and articles for personal care.

5) Be sure all bags are securely locked and that you are carrying the keys with you.

6) Do not keep all your cash in your wallet. Instead, split it up and stash some in an inside shirt pocket, separate compartment in traveling bag or pocketbook.

7) Always carry small wash n' dry packets with you for quick freshups.

8) If you should check a bag, look at the claim ticket for proper destination.

9) Tie a brightly colored string around the handle of your checked baggage for quick information in claiming.

10) Look out for signs of a delay while the plane is still at the terminal. If a flight attendant starts handing out magazines and coffee or tea, you know you are in for a long wait and mechanical trouble is the probable cause. Ask questions, especially if you have a connecting flight to make. Look for alternate carriers and get off the plane if necessary. The airline will help you if you can prove time is essential.

11) If you have not requested seat reservation before boarding, select your seat when you pick up your pass.

12) Aisle seats are good if your have long legs, like to walk around or do not like the claustrophobic feeling center seats can give.

13) Bulkhead seats usually afford more leg room than others. The

solid wall enables you to put your feet up or change positions without disturbing anyone else.

14) Seats that ride the wing are smoothest.

15) The quietest seats are usually those forward of the engine.

16) On the 727's, seats closest to the emergency exits are good as there is nothing immediately in front of you providing leg room to spare. However, since the bathrooms are nearby, be prepared for lots of traffic. Also, at high altitudes during the winter months, the draft coming through the doors is enough to turn your feet into icicles. Carry extra socks to keep the toes warm.

17) If you are on a special diet, have your travel agent request specific meals when your reservations are made.

18) Ask for a simple meal of fruit, cheese, crackers and salad as a substitute for a full course dinner if you do not like to eat a lot while flying.

19) Always carry gum to keep your throat from getting too dry and to help in popping ears at high altitudes.

20) Chocolate bars, fresh fruit or some other quick nourishment is good for a pick-me-up without having to wait for food service.

21) Do not drink alcoholic beverages excessively while in the air as one drink has the effect of two or three.

22) Water or soda is best to satisfy the thirst caused by the effects of pressurized air.

23) Yawn frequently to help relax tense throat muscles.

24) Feet swell during plane travel so try to pack a pair of folding slippers to pad around in.

25) Get up and walk about as often as you can to keep your circulation moving, especially if you are bothered by back or leg pains.

26) If your flight is long and stopovers are scheduled, make the most of the opportunity to deplane and stroll about the airport. Before deplaning, ask the attendant if there is enough time, place a seat occupied sign on your seat and carry your ticket with you. Walk around the tarmac or go to the bathroom to do a few stretching exercises. Don't however, head for the nearest bar.

27) Ask the flight attendant for a package of cards. There are many games you can play to while away your time, and you may find someone else who would like to join you in a game. It is even possible to engage in a game of cribbage, jotting your placements down on paper if you do not have a board.

28) If the plane should crash, and you survive the impact, don't

panic. Head for the nearest emergency exit. Don't stop to gather up your valuables. Leave them behind and get out of the plane as fast as you can.

29) If something should happen, keep your wits about you and carefully assess the situation. Do not make any statements unless you are sure of exactly what occurred.

30) If, for any reason, you cannot continue on, let the show chairman or someone from the club know as quickly as possible.

Traveling by Car

Going to and from shows in the family automobile is nothing new to dog people. We have all spent long hours, driven thousand of miles and endured endlessly boring superhighways in our quest to show our animals. However, once you become a judge, the task of getting to a show suddenly becomes a major undertaking. First of all, you must get there; secondly, you must be on time; and thirdly, you must not appear harassed even if you spent the last two hours trying to change a tire.

They say that getting there is half the battle, and the more you judge, the more you believe in that old axiom. It is not only necessary to have the car in tip-top working condition and know what to do if problems occur, but also know precisely where you are going. As a judge you will fervently scour maps checking on the location of the show grounds, motel/hotel and other hospitality arrangements. Some thoughtful clubs mail their judges detailed local maps showing the grounds, lodging and other places. These are terrific, but you should double check and compare route numbers and directions with a larger map to be sure everything is listed in proper sequence and location. It is a good idea to have an atlas such as the Rand-McNally *Road Atlas* on hand and better yet to have two—one for the car and the other for the house to use in checking possible mileage restrictions. If traveling by plane, photocopy the particular map that deals with the section of the state where the show is held and carry it with you. This way if you have any transportation problems, you will have more than just a vague idea of where you are going.

If you are an aspiring judge, you may be sitting back, laughing to yourself and thinking that all this is not really necessary. You naively believe that judges are wined and dined with their every whim looked after. Unfortunately this is not always true. While a great many clubs take excellent care of their judges, some do not show such concern. They may neglect to pick up the judge at the airport or take him to the show from the motel or return him. Even if he drives his own car to the show, some clubs think a judge knows exactly where the show grounds and hospitality facilities are, but this is not always true and judges are left to their own devices.

Like it or not, getting to a show is the judge's responsibility. It is great if you can depend on club members to take care of you, but be prepared to do that caring yourself. Study your maps before you leave home, have your routes well-planned and know how long it will take you to get there. Always allow at least an hour's leeway for unforeseen incidents or problems that might arise.

Your Car

There are many advantages to driving your own car to shows within a reasonable distance from home: you know its idiosyncrasies, and how it handles and operates; you know how to control it during adverse driving conditions; and you are comfortable which makes long-distance driving less tiresome than in a rented car.

Since you know you have to get where you are going within a specific length of time, make sure your car is in good working order. Either you or your garage mechanic should check all vital functions, such as oil, water, battery, belts, lights and tires. If anything is amiss, correct it before you start. Fill the tank with gas, be sure necessary maps are in the glove compartment and foul weather gear in the trunk, load your overnight bag and you are ready to depart.

Rentals

Some judges prefer to rent a car and charge the cost to the club as transportation expense. The solid reasoning behind the use of rental cars even for those shows within a moderate driving distance is that a lot of mileage can be put on a car within a year by an active judge. This may necessitate buying a new car sooner than expected, which leads to a major investment in a vehicle primarily used for doing dog shows. Also, if yours is a one-car family, the rental of a car for judging leaves the family car at home for use by others. In renting a car, you should make all reservations well in advance to procure the type and model you want. Do your best to become quickly acquainted with how the vehicle operates and keep careful track of all your expenses.

If you fly to a show, you may wish to rent a car instead of depending on club members to provide your transportation. This way there is no need to be anxious about whether you are going to be met, the time, delayed or cancelled flights or changed plans. You are totally on your own. When you make your airline reservations, line up the car as well. When you arrive at the destination airport, go to the proper car rental counter, fill out the necessary forms, pick up the keys and you are set to go. You return the vehicle back to the same airport, or another if arrangements have been made, when you are ready to depart. Travel agents are helpful in assisting you in this aspect of your itinerary.

Auto Aids

CB——Citizen Band Radios offer many advantages for those who drive long hours: the whereabouts of "Smokey," travel and road conditions, easy access to assistance if help is needed, and company for the lonely driver to name a few. Admittedly there are times when the endless chatter by the locals is boring, but you can always turn the CB down and the stereo up. Listening to truck drivers discuss their problems can be enlightening and interesting and if you are driving in other sections of the country, you can pick up local dialects. When fastening the CB in your car, use a mount that allows you to remove it easily for putting in the trunk while parked overnight in motels or hotels or at the show grounds. An antenna that retreats into the car when not in use is also a good accessory.

Gadgets——There are many items available for purchase that are designed to make driving a little easier. These range from radar detectors, FM converters, change holders and suction cups to backrests. In short, just about everything and anything is on the market. Do not outfit you car with lots of unnecessary junk, but do use those gadgets which will help make long highway hours seemingly quicker and much more comfortable.

Auto Clubs——There are many automobile clubs in existence, some regional and others national. The best known national club is AAA—Automobile Association of America, which provides its membership with 24-hour emergency road service through AAA affiliated stations, bail bonds and arrest bonds, personal accident insurance, triptiks, maps and tour books. For information about auto clubs, consult your large city yellow pages.

Problems on the Road

Flat tires, overheating, breakdowns and the like—Sinking feelings abound when the smooth-running car suddenly begins to bounce along or smoke starts rising out of the front end or just quits all together leaving you stranded on the highway. Your primary concern should be to engage all flashers and get the auto as far off the highway as possible. Once on the shoulder, assess the problem, fix it if you can or seek assistance on the local police monitored CB channel and wait for help to arrive. Tie a white handkerchief or rag to the antenna and leave the hood open to denote your status. Use flares if you do not have enough shoulder room to get the car far enough off the pavement.

Sometimes a passing motorist will stop to see if he can be of assistance, which is great if he can. However, women should be alerted for other potential problems that may arise and carefully scrutinize any would-be Samaritan. Using both sound judgment and intuition, they may have to stay in the car until bonafide help arrives especially at night.

Everyone who drives frequently should take a layman's course in auto mechanics, have proper equipment and tools in their car and carry a repair manual to guide them in either making the necessary repairs or understanding what needs to be done.

If your car breaks down and cannot be repaired within a reasonable period of time, try to rent a car to get you to the show on time.

Traffic Summons

If you are unfortunate enough to be the recipient of a traffic summons or ticket for an infraction of the law, you need to keep a cool, calm head. Do not have hysterics. Do not threaten the police officer or engage in an argument with him. And for heaven's sake, do not make a bribery attempt. All the preceding could get you into more trouble then you are already. Different states have different laws for handling traffic infractions. Try not to plead to anything until you have had the opportunity to speak with your attorney. Put up a bail bond if necessary but seek legal advice before doing anything else. Let the severity of the charge, your position and the laws of the state be your guide.

Accident

If you are involved in an accident, either a fenderbender or a much more serious one, what you can do depends on whether you are hurt. If you are hurt and are unable to get all the necessary information you need, don't worry about it. The data can be taken off the police blotter which is public record. If the accident was minor or you were not hurt, you should do the following:

a) Remain on the scene until law enforcement personnel arrives. Unless traffic is impeded, do not move your vehicle.

b) Exchange with the driver of the other car the following data: name, address, vehicle registration number, license plate number, insurance carrier, name and address of agent and code number of policy.

c) Even though no one was hurt and the cars were not seriously damaged, all parties involved must remain until the police officer arrives and makes his on-the-scene report. He may decide to issue a summons if the situation warrants one.

d) In answering any questions from a law enforcement agent, keep in mind the problem of admitting any fault that could be used against you in later court proceedings.

e) If you have any serious doubts as to your legal rights, call your family attorney and seek his advice before answering questions and signing or giving any statements to either the police or insurance investigator. In short, when in doubt keep your mouth shut before you put your foot in it.

As soon as you get home, see your insurance agent, complete insurance claim forms and motor vehicle department reports for the state in which the accident occurred. If the accident was serious, your agent or attorney will advise you as to any other steps you need to take.

If you have the accident the morning of the show and know you will be unable to continue, notify the show chairman or any available club member at once.

If You Are Delayed

If you will be late in arriving at the show grounds in time for your assignment, let someone know. If possible, contact the show chairman, hospitality chairman and so on. If you cannot find them home, they will probably already be at the show. Leave a message and ask the message taker to get word to them at once. If all else fails and you are stuck on a highway with a cop who is offering his assistance, explain your problem and ask him to radio a message into his barracks for transfer to the local police of the town in which the show grounds are situated. Usually local police help with traffic control and a message can be sent to the superintendent or show chairman in this fashion.

If you have tried everything to no avail, just sit back and wait for help. As soon as possible head for the show grounds, even if your starting time has already passed. When you get there, go at once to the superintendent's office. You may be able to pick up some of your assignment. Most clubs will delay judging a half an hour before assigning someone else to take your place. When you do arrive, you will be permitted to replace the substitute at the end of the sex or breed, depending on your overall load. Naturally, if you only had fifteen dogs or so you will probably miss the judging completely.

If you were delayed due to an accident, whether you decide to try to make the show depends not only on any injuries to you or to whoever may be accompanying you or damage to your vehicle, but also your emotional state. If you are badly shaken by the experience and you doubt your capability to function justly and properly, you would be foolish to try to judge. The exhibitors would not be getting their money's worth, and you could also blemish your reputation by making incomprehensible decisions. Sound logic based on individual personalities and the circumstances involved should prevail at all cost.

OTHER CONSIDERATIONS

Mountain Sickness

The higher you rise above sea level, the less oxygen there is in the air for you to breathe. At altitudes of five thousand feet or more

111

above sea level many people will begin to feel the effects, usually with a shortness of breath, dizziness or lack of energy. This happenstance is caused by the necessity of the heart and lungs to contract and expand more rapidly than normal to take in additional air, extract the oxygen and deliver it to other parts of the body. Adjustments will be made in vital body functions, causing a taxing of the entire system that forces a person to slow down and gradually adapt.

Judges who are not accustomed to the so-called "skinny air" could be affected by this malady. If you have any reason to believe that you may experience this sickness, set aside two or three days in advance of the show for arriving early and becoming acclimated to the air. By enjoying a mini-vacation and seeing a part of the country you are probably not familiar with, you will be giving your body a chance to adjust at the same time. Then, when you judge, you will be able to function without being too affected by the high altitude.

Heat Exhaustion

A person who is exposed to extremely high temperatures for a prolonged period of time will begin to feel the effect. Judges who are ajudicating all day long, sometimes with very little break, are particularly sensitive. Some early signals to be aware of are dizziness, vertigo, sudden weakness, nausea, dimming or blurring of vision or mild muscular cramps.

If you should feel any of these, stop judging, have your steward get the show chairman or superintendent and either take a break until you feel better or ask to be relieved from judging. Request treatment by medical personnel who may be on the grounds or, barring any trained assistance, go to a cool place to lie down, maintaining your head lower then the rest of your body and slowly sip water while ingesting salt tablets if needed.

Heat exhaustion can affect anyone at any time, but those persons not accustomed to unduly high temperatures are more apt to be bothered by them.

Any Other Illness

If at any time you feel unable to carry on judging, you should step aside. It is not inconceivable for a judge to be affected by food poisoning, climatic changes, chronic illensses and so forth, while in the ring. Heroics are neither needed nor desired, and an ill judge is doing more harm than good by trying to continue.

Exercises

To keep yourself in good health for judging, you need to eat right, sleep well and engage in a few muscle straining exercises before stepping into the ring. Unless you have done so, you can never appreciate the long hours spent in the ring, bending down zillions of times, feeling the effects the next day when you tried to get out of bed. The adjudicators who are out every weekend, keep in shape by judging. Others need to devote a few weeks before the show to an exercise program.

Exercise can take many forms and depends for a large part on your physical condition, the amount of time you are willing to spend and the type of conditioning you are interested in pursuing. Deep knee bends, touching your toes and waist twists are but some of the many exercises available that would hit the right spots: thighs, lower and upper back. Yoga and even jumping jacks are terrific for getting everything into working condition the morning of the show.

Before undertaking any physical exercise program, consult your doctor, describe the physical exertions you must go through when judging and ask him to advise a program suited to your well-being and desire.

7

The Show

Arrangements

As the show date approaches, you should receive in the mail a hospitality questionnaire, similar to the following:

ROOSEVELT KENNEL CLUB
May 20, 1981 show

Hospitality Questionnaire

1. Date of Arrival _____
   If flying: Airline _____
   Flight No. _____ Time of Arrival _____

2. Do you require transportation from the airport to the motel? _____

114

3. Do you require transportation from the motel to the show grounds? _____

4. Do you require transportation from the show grounds back to the motel? _____ to the airport? _____ If so, departure time _____ Airline _____

5. Motel Reservations are being made at the Roosevelt Motor Lodge on Route 9 (two miles north), Hyde Park, New York. Do you require a single or a double? _____ For the 19th? _____ 20th? _____

6. There will be a reception for all judges in the New Deal Room in the Motor Lodge at 6:30 p.m. on the 19th, followed by dinner at 7:30 p.m. Please indicate if you can join us:
I/We will _____ or will not _____ attend the reception and dinner.

7. Are there any other questions you may have in connection with the show?

Signed by:

_____

Return by May 1st to:
Mary Ellen Williamson
Circle Court
Hyde Park, NY 12538
914-383-9045

As you can see, this questionnaire covers all aspects of travel, lodging and social arrangements which concern the judge. The form should be completed and returned in the next mail. Be sure to keep a photostatic copy for you files.

It would be helpful if clubs would also send their judges a fact sheet containing pertinent data regarding the show, including specific details on location of show grounds and motel/hotel; cost of accommodations; if club members are not providing transportation, the distance from the airport to place of lodging with approximate cost of limo, taxi, etc.; kind of weather to expect; condition of grounds; and transportation plans for getting judges to and from the grounds.

Social Events

Many clubs take their social events very seriously. Others provide only meager functions and still others leave judges to fend for themselves. There are pluses and minuses in each case. Benefits to be derived include goodwill, understanding local practices, whether they be social, economic or political, and the opportunity to meet and talk to other judges in a relaxed atmosphere. There may be some detriments which focus on the fact that sometimes the food leaves much to be desired, speeches are too long and the evening drags on way past everyone's bedtime.

What you would wear to a social function depends entirely on whether it is formal or informal; at the motel/hotel banquet room, private house or club; and before and after the show. Common sense should guide you to something simple, classic and in good taste.

In attending club functions as a judge, it is important to remember your capacity as an adjudicator and to conduct yourself at all times in a manner befitting the position you hold. It is not wise to overindulge in alcoholic beverages. You should refrain from arguments, debates or self-serving pontifications.

Some judges absolutely abhor social functions of any description and refuse to attend, especially if they are held the evening before the show. It is not unusual for a judge to want a quiet dinner alone and go to bed early. Clubs should be understanding and not frown on this personal desire.

Getting to the Grounds

You should allow plenty of time to get to the show grounds and plan on being there at least a half an hour prior to scheduled starting time. If your are driving from home the morning of the show, map the route out in advance and be conservative about the amount of time you figure it will take you to get to the grounds. Add an additional hour for unforeseen circumstances.

If you stayed at a motel the night before and are driving yourself, be sure you received concise instructions on the whereabouts of the grounds in relation to the motel, including landmarks, mileage and estimated driving time. Verify these instructions if you have any doubts.

If you flew in and a club member or another judge will take you to the grounds, make all necessary arrangements the night before, being certain of who your driver will be and the time and place of meeting. Don't oversleep or dawdle too long in the coffee shop. Be there at the appointed hour, packed and ready to go.

If you need a ride to the show and back to the motel or airport and no one from the club has said anything to you about transportation plans, speak up. Let the show or hospitality chairman know that you need their help. Don't leave any planning until the last minute.

ON THE GROUNDS

Checking In

When you get to the grounds, check in with the superintendent or show secretary. Let the person who is marking off the judges know you are present and pick up your badge.

Judges' badges seem to come in a variety of shapes and sizes. Carefully fasten your badge to the upper left shoulder area of your jacket or dress. Some judges may have received from a previous show a special badge that denotes only their title and name. They prefer to use this one over the ordinary ribbon badges that most clubs offer. This is permissible provided the badge clearly says ''judge'' and is not ostentatious.

Casing the Ring

If you are the first person to use the ring you have been assigned for the day, case it thoroughly. Look for pieces of glass, bottle tops or other sharp objects. If indoors and matting is used, be sure the mats are laid down with the flow you have planned for your ring and that all edges are securely fastened to the floor, especially on corners and around the judge's table.

At an outdoor show, check the terrain—smooth, bumpy, level or sloping. Plan on individually gaiting your dogs on smooth, level ground. If this is not possible, establish a feeling of how dogs will move up or down hill, in or out of bumps and do everything you can to minimize the effects.

Determine the best ring layout for both the size and shape of the

117

ring and the breed or breeds you will be judging. Picture in your mind where you will have the dogs stand, the movement pattern and all-round gaiting. With a ring that is too small to accommodate all the dogs at once, you will have to establish how to split classes or eliminate animals no longer under consideration.

Check to be sure that all the needed equipment is in the ring: examining table, if one is required; numbers and award signs; judge's table and at least one chair. Your steward should already be there setting up the ribbons and handing out armbands. If you have any special instructions, advise him of your desires.

In taking over a ring from someone else, or using the ring during another judge's lunchbreak, be patient if you cannot have your ring at the allotted time. Delays can occur even though most judges try to adhere strictly to the schedule. If the only reason for the holdup is final picture taking, go ahead and step into your ring to get acclimated. Do not touch the other judge's book or personal items, but do stand there patiently. Your presence will be felt and further pictures can be taken in a free ring to enable you to start without additional delay. Never step into a ring still being used for actual judging.

What to Do When Not in the Ring

You may find yourself on the show grounds far in advance of your scheduled starting time. A beginning judge is likely to feel somewhat uncomfortable roaming about the grounds. Therefore, after checking in and casing the ring, find an inconspicuous seat either in the hospitality area or beside a ring where there are breeds being judged that you want to watch. Stay away from the benching or grooming area.

It is not necessary to totally ignore friends or give them a cold shoulder. On the other hand neither should you engage them in a conversation regardless of its innocence. A simple nod and smile should suffice. Since you are wearing your badge, they understand and will not feel slighted.

Experienced judges know that they should not watch breeds being judged that encompass a group they may be judging that day or the next. The same holds true for any breeds that they might be judging at the following show.

Spouses should stay out of the way, not engaging in conversation with possible exhibitors nor reading the catalog.

Food

Many clubs pride themselves on being able to offer the most scrumptious luncheons. A novice judge, who spent his showing days eating hardtack for hamburgers, looks forward to this repast with great relish. All too often, however, one finds that his appetite greatly diminishes as he increases his assignments.

If you are scheduled to commence judging a short assignment around lunch time, have a light snack before going into the ring. Don't try to judge on a full stomach, especially if you are apt to be somewhat nervous.

The half hour allotted for lunch during a full day's judging is quickly whittled away by posing for pictures, a trip to the bathroom and giving your book to the superintendent for safe-keeping while out of the ring. These activities leave only ten or fifteen minutes for lunch. Therefore, wise judges will eat a large breakfast and depend on a light noontime meal to sustain them throughout the day.

A few judges who do not like to break concentration, prefer not to leave their ring for anything other than a quick trip to the bathroom. Their steward or someone from the hospitality committee brings a light lunch to them on request.

Many clubs send hospitality members around frequently during the day bearing coffee or tea if it is cold, or lemonade or iced tea if it is hot. Alcohol should never be consumed while judging or in the midst of a break. Cigarettes should only be smoked during free periods.

Judge's Emergency Kit

Unless you are judging a breed that attracts high entries, your initial assignments will not be very long. Be sure to bring at least two ballpoint pens, breed standards and the AKC Rules and Regulations. These items can be carried in a pocket, handbag or durable, waterproof pouch.

For a long assignment, you may want to bring along extra articles to see you through any possible happenstance. These items can include anything from headache and stomach pills, bee sting swabs to a quick fix for a stocking run or torn pants. Since you have very little time to spend on yourself, you will feel more comfortable if you have just about everything you may need readily available. Naturally if your spouse accompanies you and is not judging, this emergency kit can be his/her responsibility. Otherwise you will have to plan in advance exactly what you may need.

Posing For Pictures

Posing for pictures is one aspect of judging that every adjudicator anticipates with either relish or chagrin. If you are comfortable with having your picture taken, then you will not mind when asked to pose by an exhibitor or handler with his winning dog. You will regard this question with dismay, however, if you are unsure of the most advantageous way to present yourself before a camera.

Pictures should only be taken at the end of a time period or an assignment to avoid delays during an hour's schedule. If the ring has to be used by another judge, then suggest that the picture be taken elsewhere to avoid holding up the next adjudicator.

To assist you in making the most of your pictures, here are photographs and tips on proper standing and kneeling positions. Jayne Langdon, a noted California photographer who has lectured on the subject, took these pictures of multi-group judge Edd E. Bivin.

The proper stance for most judges is standing upright with the body turned slightly towards the camera, leading with the right shoulder and leg. The degree of turn depends on whether one is heavy, skinny or any variation in between. This three-quarter presentation is comfortable when weight is placed on the left leg letting the right on relax and bend slightly from the knee. Feet should be set apart and angled. Ribbons held at their ends with fingertips using the right hand for the top and left for the bottom, slanting the ribbons counterclockwise at about 11 and 5 o'clock.

When kneeling the same theories apply except that judges must avoid appearing as if they are ready to catch a baseball. Knees should be brought as close as possible while still maintaining balance. Three-quartered turn also applies when kneeling with the degree of turn depending on one's size. A heavier person would present more of a side view than one who has little bulk.

Whether one looks at the dog or over the photographer's shoulder depends on personal preferences and appearance. Some people are more comfortable with a side view looking down at the dog and yet others appear more attractive looking towards the photographer. Glare from glasses presents a problem at indoor shows when a flash is used. Try to look at a slight angle away from the camera rather then

Bivin demonstrates a modified three-
~~quar~~ter stance with his weight on his left leg
~~whi~~le his right shoulder and leg lead toward
camera. *Jayne Langdon*

Edd's kneeling position features a slight turn
toward the camera with his right side. *Jayne
Langdon*

121

directly into it. If possible, dark glasses should be removed. Smiling or not is a matter of personal preference.

Dog show photographers trying to get the best pictures they can will direct judges on where they should be, whether to stand or kneel, and where to place large trophies. Photographers have to account for not only the size of the dog, handler and judge, but also to take under consideration the dog's color and the color of clothes worn by the people in the picture. It is easy to lose a dark dog in dark clothing. Similarly, light blends with light and the dog will not show up sufficiently.

A judge is always asked if a picture can be taken and is under no obligation to agree. If the dog fits the win, then a picture memento is treasured by all. On the other hand pictures of a fourth place win in the classes at a non-specialty event serve no purpose.

Taking a cigarette break during judging is taxing on both the exhibitors and their dogs. *Cummin —GAZETTE, American Kennel Club*

8

Ring Procedure

***

STEPPING INTO THE RING, you are the only one who knows if you are prepared to adjudicate. If you are not ready your actions, or lack thereof, will quickly reveal insecurity and indecisiveness. Similarly if you possess the necessary knowledge, talent and acumen the manner in which you conduct yourself and your ring will apprise all of your ability.

Physical aspects of ring control should be second nature and not confused with mental evaluations. All steps need to be kept at a minimum so plan your ring procedure with this thought in mind. If a table breed, the table should be handy, yet out of the way. Individual examination, stacking and gaiting patterns for each animal should occur in the exact same spot with subsequent dogs moving up as the preceding one is being evaluated. By pre-establishing a simple and concise method of ring control for most average conditions and entries, your physical actions should require little further thought.

Average Class Size

As the first class comes into the ring, you should instruct either the exhibitors or the stewards if you have knowledgeable people assisting you, where you want the dogs to line up. Preferably this is to the side of the entrance gate with all dogs facing counterclockwise. Make note of any absentees and be sure that armband numbers correspond with those listed for that class in the judge's book. Walk alongside the animals mentally measuring the standing quality of the class. Then ask the group to go around in a circle, either once or twice depending on the size of dogs, the ring and the number of entries. Instruct the exhibitor of the first dog where you want him to stop. A table breed's stopping point should be adjacent to the table. In other breeds, this point would be at the beginning of the individual gaiting pattern.

Table breeds sometimes require a little extra patience and understanding. Some owners have not adequately trained their dog to hold still for examination on the table and the judge needs to be firm yet gentle in guiding the dog into a reasonable stance for examination.

Whether the dog is on the table or on the ground, you want all four feet standing firm, with the body pulled together, head and tail in proper position. Nothing could be worse than trying to examine an animal that looks like it will collapse into a heap at the slightest provocation.

Step back from the animal and view it overall before you begin to assess him with hands. As you approach offer the front side of your hand as a means of letting him know that you mean no harm and to get some indication of his reaction to you. Keep yourself tuned into the mental condition of the dog at all times. Anne Rogers Clark, prominent judge and former handler, describes this process when she says, ''I want a dog to look at me and to feel that there is somebody behind those eyes. That he knows what's going on. By looking a dog in the eye and judging its expression you have some idea of what kind of temperament it has. Is it friendly? Is it kindly? Should you be careful of it? Is it going to bite? Do you hear a rumble? Does the dog look at you kind of funny, like 'I don't know whether I want you to put your hands on me or not?' . . . I narrowly missed some very bad bites and missed them because I had an inkling that something was going to happen. So, I think you have to be a little cautious. You have to do a little reading of the dog and the person who is showing the dog. Are they aware of it?''

If you feel that he is about to bite, either because the animal is tensing or growling outright, be sure the person on the other end of the lead has a firm grip on his head. If you believe you are going to encounter some problems instruct the exhibitor to control his dog. Don't wait until you have been bitten.

Before physically going over any animal be sure the exhibitor has a firm command of his charge. Be tuned in for possible reactions and avoid sudden movements that might startle the dog. Once you have started, try to keep at least one hand always touching the animal's body as some dogs need reassurance of constant contact until the entire examination procedure is over. This can be difficult, however, with nervous exhibitors who stand glued to the spot forcing you to move away from the dog and around him in order to reach the center body and rear structure.

The method of examination favored by most judges starts at the head, working downwards and backwards until ending with the tail. Let your hands gently, but firmly, feel what you may or may not be able to see with your eyes. Check the head, bite and ears before moving to the shoulders, front legs and feet. Next comes the body, spring of ribs and rise, if one is called for. Then the animal's rear, loin, tail and testicles, if a male. It is not necessary to emphasize the use of your hands as your motions should be quick and smooth. Step back and take a second look if you wish.

Instruct the exhibitor to move his dog in whatever pattern you have established. While this dog is moving the next animal should be setting up or put on the table for individual examination. The dog you are individually gaiting should be evaluated, regaited if necessary, and then positioned either at the end of the line or in a new line that you will form on the opposite side of the ring. As each dog is individually examined and gaited, he should be placed in this new line according to the approximate placement in the class. Don't be afraid to ask someone to move forward or backward to make room for a newcomer.

After you have gone over all the dogs, you should have them closely positioned as to your assessment of class placements. You may wish to make a change or two. A preliminary standing is not a permanent one and is therefore subject to whatever changes you deem necessary. When you are satisfied, ask the class to go around the ring again for an overall view, make position changes if required, and in going by, you point and say number one to the first dog, two to the second, three to the third and four to the fourth. Make a final check on absentees, mark your book and hand out the ribbons. By positioning the dogs in order of merit and then adhering to this system, there can be little confusion on the part of the exhibitors or the ringside as to your placements.

Large Classes

Large numbered entries in singular classes require certain additional methods. In fact, you may discover that you are judging classes within a class in order to give each dog equal opportunity and fair evaluation. The basics remain the same as those adopted for small classes, but have to be repeated as you break down the class size into separate, manageable forms.

Initially assemble the entire class into the ring. Let the dogs form circles within circles if need be. Check off armbands and make note of absentees. Count the total number present and split the class into as many equal segments as practicable to permit the dogs to move around the ring without stepping on each other or interfering with your full view of the animals. You also need to be sure that you will have enough room to individually examine and gait each dog. Assuming there is room, detain the dogs you are not using in a corner of the ring. Instruct the exhibitors of dogs not currently being evaluated to let their animals relax. There are three main reasons for wanting to keep the entire class in the ring:

1) All dogs are there and present so you will not have to wait for them to be collected or rounded up when you need them.

2) A ringer cannot be substituted.

3) An animal originally present cannot out of the blue be mysteriously absent.

If you have to temporarily excuse dogs from the ring because there is not sufficient room, be sure to make proper note of all armband numbers and have the dogs and their exhibitors/handlers wait adjacent to the ring.

If you do not like the idea of initially assembling all the dogs of a large class in the ring and either having some of the animals tuck themselves into a corner or sending them temporarily outside to wait for their turn, there is another option. Namely, you can separate an extremely large class before the dogs even come into the ring by telling the steward that you only want the first ten dogs, catalog numbers blank through blank, in the ring. Proceed to judge these animals and keep the best five, having them stand in a corner of the ring. Then ask the steward for the next ten. Judge this lot and excuse all but those you deem equal to or better than the first five standing at ease in a corner. Have these remainders, if any, stand with the others and continue to segment and judge the rest of the class. Once you have gone over all the dogs and excused those you are no longer interested in, you should have remaining in the corner the dogs under contention for placements. Quickly reevaluate as needed, sort through them and designate placements as you would with an ordinary sized class. Be sure to make note of any absentees as you go along.

If you find the above method too awkward and would prefer to judge all dogs of a given class as an entire unit, then you may want to adopt the system of using a scrap piece of paper to keep track of evaluations. As each animal is individually examined and gaited, sort them out by making notes on the paper of your assessments of the animal's quality. Such a method might be something along this line: write down the corresponding armband number and put a symbol next to it, such as an ''A'' for excellent, ''B'' for good, ''C'' for fair and ''D'' for poor. Use pluses and minuses if you wish to denote deviations from the norm. This method indicates overall positive judging as opposed to negative judging where you may want to symbolize on specific points such as bite, head, structure, movement and so forth.

After you have gone over every entrant in the class, gather all the dogs in the ring once more, check your symbols and begin eliminating from the ring those that will not be in further contention. Always keep no less than six dogs in case one of the animals should pull up lame. What you should be left with is the highest rated dogs which you may want to quickly reevaluate to refresh your memory and place in position according to your findings. Let the dogs proceed around the ring to enable you to get a sweeping appraisal. If you are satisfied make no further changes in the line-up and as they go by you, place the class.

By segmenting large entry classes you can accomplish three vital purposes:

1) All animals receive equal treatment under like conditions and circumstances.

2) There is enough room for each dog to be fully evaluated.

3) You would not be likely to become confused and lost in the mire of a vast maze of dogs.

Variances

There are many physical variances that every judge may adopt. Here are some ideas for consideration:

a) For specific instructions that vary from the norm, assemble all the exhibitors in the class around you and tell them what you expect them to do. For example, if you are only going to gait three dogs around the ring at a time, let them know. Advise them as a group and you will save time, be less likely to lose your concentration and avoid having to monotonously repeat the same instructions.

b) Large dogs that need room to fully stride may be segmented regardless of the number of animals in the class. Let each dog go around the ring by himself or take three dogs at a time for comparison purposes.

c) Have the dogs line up in catalog order. This serves the function of making it easier for you to determine which animal began the line, removes any possibility of jockeying for position by handlers and gives everyone an equal opportunity.

d) If you wish to have a dog gait again after having conducted your preliminary examinations, ask its exhibitor to come to you as you stand at the head of your gaiting pattern, which permits every animal to be gaited in the exact same spot, under identical terrain and conditions.

e) Use your initial go-around to check for possible size disqualifications and lameness as well as allowing the dogs to settle down and get accustomed to the ring.

f) If you have a problem with a particular dog, give it every chance to adhere to your basic requirements. If you still cannot examine the animal to your satisfaction, excuse it from the ring.

Judging Winners and Reserve

Armband numbers need to be verified against the book for Winners Dog or Bitch and reserve classes. It is not necessary to completely reexamine every dog in the ring since you had already done so in the winning classes. Having the dogs circle the ring together and then individually gaiting them will usually suffice in jogging your memory. If there is a particular aspect, however, that needs closer attention, then recheck that point. When you are satisfied, award your Winners, mark the book and hand out the ribbon before moving on to Reserve.

If the Winners was alone in his breed class, you can automatically award Reserve Winners. However, if not, then the dog that placed second to the Winners must be brought into the ring for Reserve Winners judging. It is not necessary to totally rejudge the entire

Reserve class, instead have the newcomer individually gait, make your assessment of him against the competition in the ring, reevaluate other dogs in the ring and render your decision.

Best of Breed/Variety and Best of Winners

Your Best of Breed Class is unique as the dogs assembled before you include not only your Winners Dog and Winners Bitch but also animals that have already attained their championship. You need to remember, however, that just because a dog is a champion does not mean that he has the edge on the class dogs. Every dog should be appraised, regardless of titles, as he appears that day with no consideration for past wins, records or other consideration.

In this class the dogs and bitches are combined together. Some judges prefer to separate the sexes and others do not. Regardless of your preferences, the Best of Breed Class should be considered the same as every other class you have judged that day. Your purpose is to select the Best of Breed dog, the Best of Winners and the Best of Opposite Sex following the same procedure you adopted for your class judging. Individually examine, gait, appraise and sort through all the dogs, positioning them in some semblance of order according to your judgment of their merit. Don't leave the Winners Dog and Bitch out in the cold. While it is not necessary to totally reexamine these two, they deserve more than a cursory glance. If they are of sufficient quality to be considered for Best of Breed, then by all means give them due consideration.

When you have made your determinations, put the potential Best of Breed dog first in line, followed by the Best of Winners and Best of Opposite Sex. Take the class around reviewing your positions. If satisfied, place them in that order, mark your book and hand out the ribbons.

Group and Best in Show Judging

When you judge the group your basic judging pattern will be the same as used in regular classes. You must initially account for, examine, gait and assess each dog as you evaluate them against your interpretations of their standards. It is only after going down the whole line, however, that you will want to pull out and position those dogs you are interested in. With large groups you may want to excuse the animals that are not in contention. Your steward can do this upon your instructions. If you do eliminate, be sure that you have left in the ring no fewer than six dogs in case one becomes lame or you have to excuse a dog for some other reason. When you have made your determination, position the animals in a line in accordance with your judgment, take them around, speak and point to your number one, two, three and four. Mark the placements in your judge's book, verify all absentees and hand out the ribbons.

Best in Show procedure closely follows that of a small class, except there is no reason to position the six dogs. You are only looking for one animal to award the top prize. Some judges like to build up the suspense at large shows by marking their book before letting the exhibitor and spectators know who their winner is.

Gaiting Patterns

There are four principal gaiting patterns:

Triangle——The most popular pattern due to the fact that it enables the judge to see the dog's front, rear and side action in an unbroken stride.

L-shaped——This pattern permits viewing of both sides of the dog on the top of the upsidedown "L" as the exhibitor usually switches the lead from his left to his right hand as he turns. The advantage of being able to see both sides rests primarily with a dog that has uneven or unsightly markings on one side which may detract from his other merits if that is the only side which is viewed.

Down and Back——The simplest of all, a straight line away from and back to the judge, this pattern emphasizes on only front and rear action.

Circle——Usually used in conjunction with any of the above, the circle allows the dog to gait smoothly and clearly regardless of ring size.

The pattern you decide to use will depend on the size of the ring, terrain, number of dogs and specific breed. A small ring may not lend itself to anything other than straight up and down with a following circle. An outdoor show featuring woodchuck holes leads one to determine the best layout based on the smoothest turf that can be found in the ring.

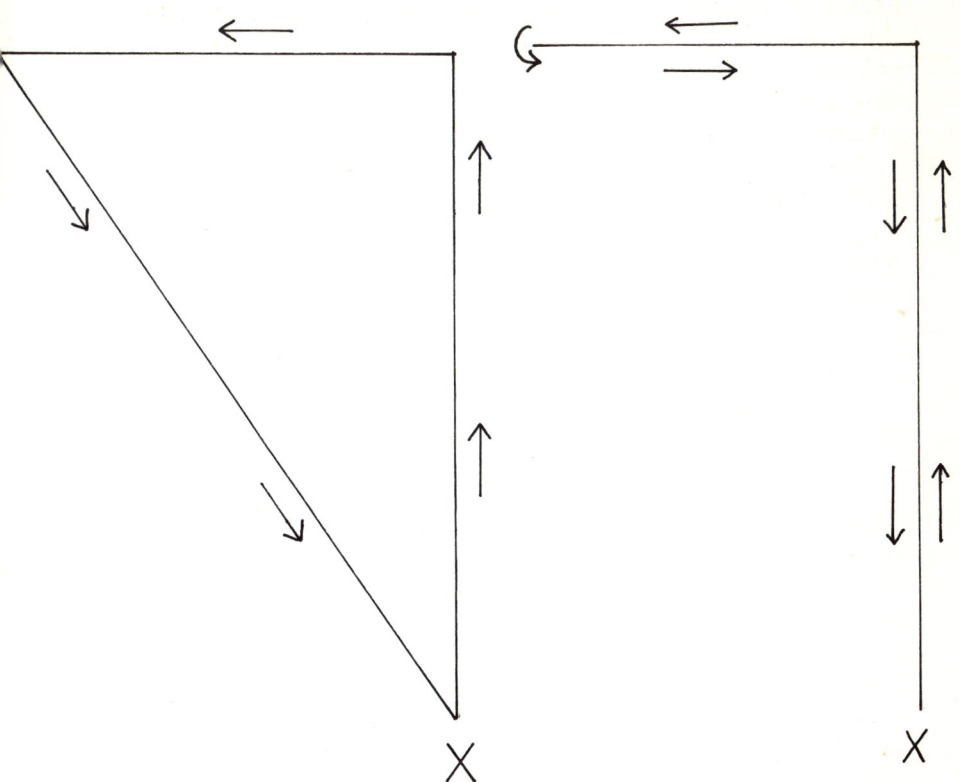

"Triangle" lets the judge observe movement down, across and back in an unbroken stride.

"L-shaped" pattern is used by those who want to be able to view both sides of the animal moving.

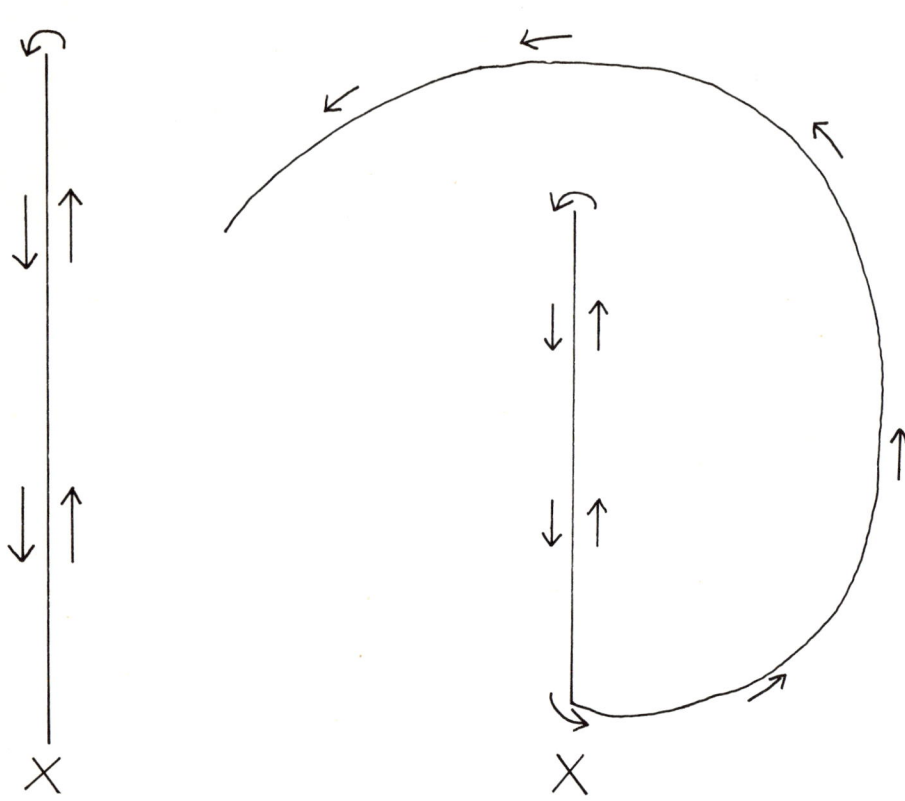

**"Down and Back"
is a simple coming
and going pattern.**

**The "Circle" may follow any of the other patterns and is
especially useful in a small or crowded ring.**

Giving Instructions

When talking with an exhibitor, it is necessary to keep comments to a bare minimum. Your words can be easily misconstrued by both the person you are speaking with and the spectators outside the ring.

You should not ask any questions, nor seek any suggestions. If you want to know the animal's age, have the steward check in the catalog and give you the date of birth.

All vocal instructions must be kept clear, simple and to the point. As the voice does not always carry, hand signals are a prerequisite for every judge. They do not have to be elaborate nor theatrical. Rather they should be natural, straightforward and easy to decipher.

Change of Handler and Late Dogs

It is a judge's prerogative as to whether he wishes to allow a change of handlers or late dogs in his ring while a class is still in progress. The steward, having been apprised of the situation by the exhibitor, will ask the judge for his permission before any changes or additions can be made. A simple yes or no is all that is necessary. Nevertheless no handler changes may be made if the judge has already individually examined and individually gaited all the dogs currently in the ring. Technically, late dogs may be permitted up until the book is marked.

The Judge's Book

As with all other physical aspects of judging, marking your book should become second nature. Markings need to be clear and accurate so that there can be no misunderstandings as to your decisions. It is best to use a ballpoint pen being sure to press down so that all copies are carboned.

The book is comprised of a front cover which lists your assignments, time and segment covered therein, questions on correctly marking the book, a certification and place for your signature. Contained in the book are the breed sheets, the original of which is white and three copies. More than one sheet may cover a breed depending on the number of entries and policy of the superintendent who makes

JUDGE'S BOOK

Name of Club ROOSEVELT KENNEL CLUB

Date May 20, 1981

Judge John Q. Judge

Ring Number 5   **Scheduled Judging Time** 9:00 AM

Total Number of Dogs to be Judged 64

BREEDS

9:00 AM	-	11 Bichon Frise
		14 Dalmatians
10:00 AM	-	12 Keeshonden
		~~13 Chow Chows~~
11:00 AM	-	35 Lhasa Apsos

Time Started _____ **Time Finished** _____

JUDGE'S CERTIFICATION

Have you entered time started and time finished? _____

Have you marked all absentees? _____

Have you marked ALL CLASSES correctly, including catalog numbers of Winners, Reserve, Best of Breed (Variety), Best of Winners, and Best of Opposite Sex? _____

_____
Signature of Judge

Cover of a judge's book showing the Judge's Certification which must be signed upon completion of the assignment contained therein.

134

BREED OR VARIETY   DALMATIANS — DOGS   JUDGE

PUPPY DOGS		NOVICE DOGS		BRED BY EXHIBITOR DOGS		AMERICAN-BRED DOGS		OPEN DOGS	
CATALOG NUMBER	AWARD	CATALOG NUMBER	AWARD	CATALOG NUMBER	AWARD	CATALOG NUMBER	AWARD	CATALOG NUMBER	AWARD
5	1			17	2			9	3
15	Dis. Breed standard SBT			1st withheld lack of merit SBT				11	1
								13	2

WINNERS DOG   *11*   RESERVE   *13*

```
XXXXXXXXXXXXXXXXXXXXXXXXXXXXXXXXXXXXXXXXXXXXXXXXXXXXXX
XXXXXXXXXXXXXXXXXXXXXXXXXXXXXXXXXXXXXXXXXXXXXXXXXXXXXX
XXXXXXXXXXXXXXXXXXXXXXXXXXXXXXXXXXXXXXXXXXXXXXXXXXXXXX
XXXXXXXXXXXXXXXXXXXXXXXXXXXXXXXXXXXXXXXXXXXXXXXXXXXXXX
```

TIME: START *9:20*   FINISH_____

— PLEASE USE BALL POINT PEN —

Sample marking for males.

DALMATIANS — BITCHES   JUDGE

PUPPY BITCHES		NOVICE BITCHES		BRED BY EXHIBITOR BITCHES		AMERICAN-BRED BITCHES		OPEN BITCHES	
CATALOG NUMBER	AWARD	CATALOG NUMBER	AWARD	CATALOG NUMBER	AWARD	CATALOG NUMBER	AWARD	CATALOG NUMBER	AWARD
16	1	8	Disq. measured out SBT					6	1
								12	excused lame sbt
								18	2

WINNERS BITCH   16   RESERVE   6

ENTERED FOR BEST OF BREED (VARIETY) COMPETITION

7 (d)
10 (b)
14 (d) abs

BEST OF BREED OR VARIETY
NO. 7
BEST OF WINNERS
NO. 11
BEST OF OPPOSITE SEX
NO. 10

TIME: START_____   FINISH 9:59   AMERICAN KENNEL CLUB COPY

Sample markings for bitches and intersex.

136

up the book. At the bottom of each sheet is a place for making note of the time you began and finished that respective breed.

Once you have placed your dogs and they are standing next to the correct placemarkers, write down the placings opposite the exhibitors' armband numbers and hand out the ribbons. Check for absentees that you may not have recorded during the initial entrance. It is good practice for a judge to place armbands that have not been picked up for a class currently in progress on top of the breed sheet. Then, if late comers arrive, the judge does not have to stop judging and correct his book. Also when the time comes for marking the book, the absentees can be readily accounted for.

If a dog is excused or disqualified, notation should be made of this decision together with the reason next to the number assigned to that animal. If there are any other unusual circumstances that need to be recorded, the book should indicate such occurrences. If statements are made, they should be kept short and to the point.

Any errors that occur in typesetting the book should be corrected by the superintendent, who determines the facts, checks the entries if necessary and places his initials next to the correction.

If you made a mistake in your placement markings or if a dog marked absent appears and is still eligible for competition, all you need to do is make the corrections and place your initials adjacent to any changes you made.

Marking the judge's book is not difficult. A few suggestions are listed below to assist you.

a) Mark class placements with a 1, 2, 3 or 4.

b) Mark Winners Dog, Winners Bitch, Reserves, Best of Breed/ Variety, Best of Winners and Best Opposite Sex with the armband number that corresponds with the winning dog.

c) Put time for starting and ending each breed at the bottom of the first and last page covering that breed.

d) If you withhold a ribbon, state what you withheld with an indication as to why, such as lack of merit.

e) Always check your book over for errors when you finish each breed.

f) If something was out of order and was not caught beforehand, expect to receive a letter from the AKC Show Records Department, requesting clarification.

g) If, after returning home and marking your catalog from your copy of the sheets, you notice an error, call the AKC and follow up with a written explanation.

9

The Mental Process

T HE MOST ARDUOUS PART of judging is not the physical actions necessitated by what you do and how you do it. The real challenge lies with the mental process you must develop in reaching just and equitable decisions. It is what you think in your head that needs to take command, not what you are suppose to do with your body. For this reason ring procedure must become secondary and automatic. If you have to stop and think about what you are suppose to be doing at any given point, then you run the risk of completely losing the concentration that good judgments demand.

You need to be conscious of your thought waves, the shifting of mental patterns and considering various elements as you weigh one point against another as well as one dog against both its standard and the competition of the day. This process, not to be taken lightly, dictates that you devote time in carefully preparing yourself for the task that will confront you. Education and comprehension must be current and ongoing, as you arm yourself with a thorough knowledge of anatomy, breed standards, history and individual breed idiosyncrasies, together with a total understanding of the mental process required in reaching judicial determinations.

Anatomy

Every mammal has the same basic anatomical structure, but each species varies from that basic form to comprise separate and distinctive animals. Similarly dogs follow this trait with the formation of specific breeds, which are still composed of the same essential structure. A judge should have at least an elementary understanding of structure and its effect in order to totally comprehend the reasons why an individual dog may look and move as it does. This knowledge enables the adjudicator to translate what he finds upon examining and gaiting a dog into useful information for a proper evaluation of the animal.

Available are several excellent books, dealing with this subject in depth, which should be studied. But some of the best illustrations covering different anatomical layers within a single dog are those prepared by Robert F. Way, VMD, MS. See the illustrations by Dr. Way reproduced on the end sheets inside the front cover of this book. Carefully study them and become fully aware of the relationship between what you see and feel in the general outline of a dog and what actually exists beneath in bone structure.

Movement

You cannot thoroughly study the anatomical structure of a dog without piecing together in your mind the way that animal would move. Gait and structure go hand and hand and must be contemplated as joint units.

Not all breeds move alike and as a judge you need to understand exactly how the breed you are judging should move. What may be good for a Gordon Setter is obviously not good for a Bloodhound and the reasons for the differences in movement lie within the basic structure variances comprising the two breeds.

Some judges ask to have the dogs move at a walk, but this can make dogs not accustomed to gaiting in the ring appear awkward and cumbersome. Most judges like to see the trot when individually moving dogs. This gait may vary in speed from slow to fast trotting and the judge should let the exhibitor know if the speed is too fast or too slow.

In watching a dog move you should be aware of the common gaiting problems that exist. These faults are usually found in every

139

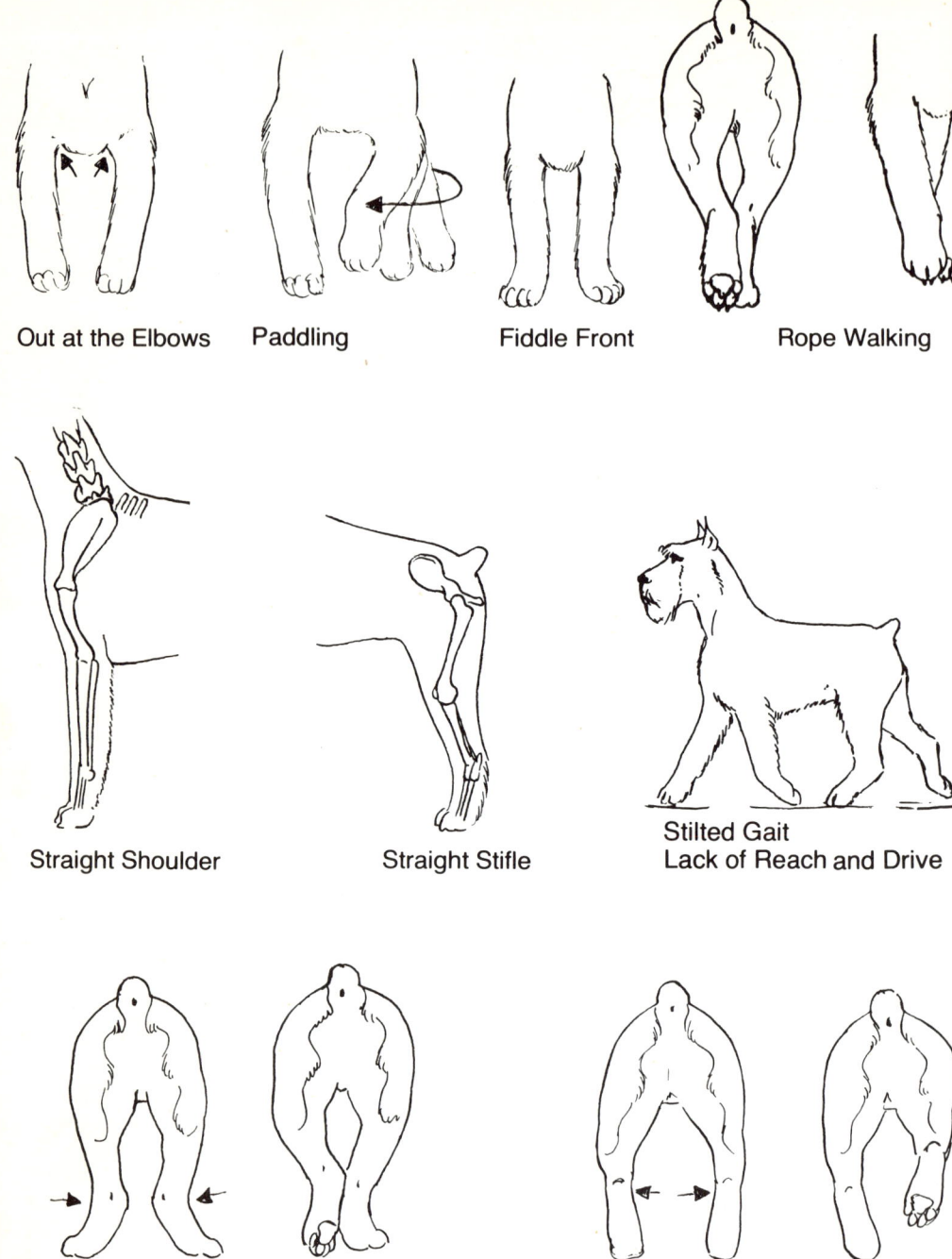

Out at the Elbows   Paddling   Fiddle Front   Rope Walking

Straight Shoulder   Straight Stifle   Stilted Gait
                                                  Lack of Reach and Drive

Cow-Hocked   Open Hocked

All drawings on these pages are by Gail B. Mackiernan and reproduced from *The Standard Schnauzer Illustrated.*

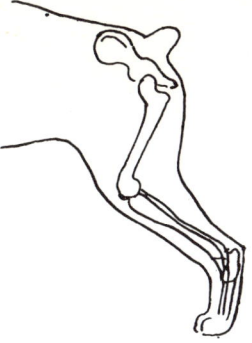

Over-angulated
Stifle

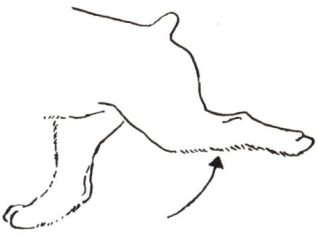

High-Kicking
Rear Movement

The ideal stance

The ideal movement

breed and must be correctly assessed when they are noticed. Also a good movement in one breed may be prohibitive in another. There are many excellent publications and materials that thoroughly analyze these problems.

In observing a dog standing naturally and subsequently watching him move, you should be able to see a correlation between incorrect structure and gait.

Standards and Histories

It is almost impossible to adequately translate the written standard into a visual concept without also delving into the breed history: written words only paint a very broad picture of the animal. You need to know the breed's purpose, background and heritage in order to be able to fill in any gaps that may occur in composing that picture.

Once you have read the history, look at the standard. Try to mentally develop a concise image of the breed drawing upon all the factors you have digested. If you have difficulty in clearly delineating certain portions, do further research. Although standards are suppose to be the bible which guides the judge in forming correct opinions regarding breed type, many standards leave much to be desired in this regard. Not only are the terms subject to dissimilar interpretations, but on occasions the picture painted from a strict understanding of the words could give you an animal that would be far afield from the breed likeness intended. You should also be aware of any unwritten components that have passed down through the years and yet never find themselves included in the official breed standard.

An excellent source that you should explore in learning more about the breed is the national breed club. Some of the national clubs have published illustrated and written studies of their respective standards. These booklets are the result of many long hard hours spent by breed aficionados in recognizing that greater assistance is needed in guiding judges to a better understanding of their breed.

National clubs will also write to approved judges of their breed advising them of traits or trends that are detrimental to the breed. Letters can cover anything from coat length, trim and texture, to topline and movement. They serve as reminders to judges about factors that the clubs feel are being ignored. The idea is to get the judges back on the right track and not let popular traits develop to a point that the original designs of the breed become obliterated.

Some breed clubs also sponsor symposiums focusing on their breeds. The success of any forum depends on program quality, lack of dominance by one clique or another and sincerity in honestly explaining and adhering to the standard. Well-thought-out seminars offer true opportunities for learning various aspects about breeds and how they should be correctly judged. Many judges will make note of the major elements by underlining them in their books of standards. Others make up their own review cards: synopsis of the standard, including major and minor faults and disqualifications.

Mentally Evaluating the Dogs

Armed with all of the above material and having reviewed the breed standard, AKC rules and your ring procedure the night before, you are ready mentally to evaluate the dogs that enter your ring.

When you look at the animals, you are measuring them against the image you have painted of the perfect specimen of the breed and against each other, determining your placements in order of their respective merits. Be on guard for obvious disqualifications and weigh in your mind overall quality versus faults. Totally concentrate on the dogs before you, gradually weeding through class after class, section after section until you come up with your major winners. This process is not a difficult one if you came into the ring prepared to evaluate the dogs justly. It does, however, become extremely laborious if you cannot divorce yourself from outside influential factors: such as heavily advertised dogs, animals owned or shown by friends or enemies, dogs handled by recognized top handlers, animals you have previously favored with wins, and so on down through a long list of biases that should never enter your mind when judging dogs.

Most of the judges who are labeled as being blatantly dishonest are in fact lacking in the knowledge, expertise and courage that good decisions require. Do not let yourself fall into this trap.

Natural vs. Educated Eye

What is the so-called "eye"? Why is having one such an important plus? Must you be born with an eye or can it be carefully nurtured?

The eye is a term given to describe one's innate ability consistently and easily to choose quality animals of any breed without becoming bogged down in semantics. If you have a natural eye at a first glance you can disconcern which dogs are in the running and which are not. Correct breed type and structure come automatically to mind without even thinking about them. This is a great advantage when you are judging because you immediately know which dogs you have to choose for a closer look and evaluation. It matters not if you have one dog or a hundred, you can quickly and accurately assess quality and type.

Some say the eye comes naturally from within, while others maintain that through careful study and education the eye can evolve into existence. It is hoped that the latter is true because very few persons have an innate eye and the majority who do not need to have some encouragement.

There are many judges in the ring today who do not have a natural eye. There are also many who recognize this factor and strive to offset the lack of connate ability with the desire methodically and carefully to evaluate the dogs that come before them. Some are successful and yet others become completely mired in quicksand.

If you do not possess a natural eye, do not be dejected. You can develop a close resemblance to what comes naturally to others if you have the necessary self-esteem, intelligence and desire. Your judging may be slower and more analytic than that of your natural counterpart, but as long as your conjectures are justifiably accurate this should not disturb you at all.

Positive vs. Negative Judging

When you look at a dog do you automatically think first of his faults? Or is it the good points that capture your mind? Do you weigh one against the other? Or can you not see the virtue of the plus points through the obvious deviations of the minus?

Judging should always be approached in the positive. It is not what you do not like about a particular dog that counts, rather it should be those elements that really capture your eye and lead you to place that animal. Similarly you should not refuse to evaluate a dog because of a glaring fault. Unless the fault is such that it would require disqualification, you need fairly to appraise the entire dog before you can determine any measure of its overall quality. To zero in on one, and only one, negative aspect is to completely ignore the total picture. Therefore all judging should be determined from a positive viewpoint.

Fault Judging

To reject a dog solely on the negative leads to fault judging, which should be avoided at all cost. Every dog has defects or faults—no animal is perfect—and the emphasis placed on that fault depends on the judgment of the person officiating. The pitfalls lie when you judge solely on a particular fault to the detriment of whatever good points may be present.

It is not at all uncommon for a breeder-judge to heavily penalize a dog that has a fault he saw most often in his own lines, or for the unsure judge to fluctuate between different faults from one weekend to the next, usually based on the input he received from outside persons who say that this, that or the next fault is the biggest problem facing the breed.

Melbourne T.L. Downing, an all-breed judge with considerable experience, gives emphasis to the above when he states, "It would be wrong to discard a dog that has an obvious fault instead of judging the whole dog. Sometimes the dog with an obvious fault when candidly analyzed turns out to be a rather good dog that maybe can contribute much to the breed. So be careful about the dog that has an obvious fault."

You are not in the ring to pick out the animal with the least amount of faults, nor the one without a specific fault. Your job is to choose the dog that best measures up to your interpretation of the breed standard: an animal that exemplifies type, balance, condition and quality. If you mentally function in this fashion you will not fall into the trap of becoming overly critical because of one specific fault or another.

Type

Clearly defining type has been described by many as difficult. This is because there are two versions as to what exactly represents type. One school of thought rests with the idea that there is a single breed type which is the definition of the standard. Others say that there may be several types within a breed based on solid distinctions that have been passed along with years of inbreeding one line or another. There is reason to agree with both thoughts.

Type is the standard. It is the exemplification of exactly what the specific breed should look like and major deviations therefrom bring

146

about a dog that is farther away from the physical structure that makes each breed separate and distinctive.

Many breeds through years of careful, guarded linebreeding, with occasional outcrosses have produced different appearances within the allotted breed type. It is not unusual to look at a certain dog and be able to tell what his bloodlines are and where he came from. In this particular dog a clear, definitive appearance differs from that of his neighbor as many different strains can appear within a single breed. Such differences are generally qualified with the word type. This is a misnomer. It is better to define the differences that occur within a breed as those being representative of the standard with internal variations. These variations will not alter the overall appearance, or type, which clearly defines that specific breed.

Condition and Showmanship

While you are trying mentally to determine the importance of type, structure and gait, there are two other thoughts you should consider: condition and showmanship.

Condition describes the general good health and well-being that is expected of every show dog. The animal must be of sufficient weight for his size and build, have good muscle tone and possess a clean, shiny coat. If it is a medium or long-haired dog, the coat should have the proper texture, trim and profusion as required by the standard. Conditioning is important because it enables the judge to see the dog in top form and to analyze it correctly without obvious distractions.

Showmanship is another matter to be weighed. A natural showman possesses an elusive element which sets him apart from the competition. This dog immediately draws the judge to him even though his quality may be fair in all other respects. Showmanship then becomes something to be guarded against as you would not want to put a dog up merely because he is on his toes.

Similarly you do not want to overlook a good animal because he does not show well and lets everyone know his obvious displeasure at being in the ring; nor the dog whose exhibitor has no idea as to what is going on and is too nervous to show his pet to its best advantage.

Ideally a great show dog needs to have these essential components: he must have type, be well-balanced and sound; he should be properly conditioned and handled; he needs to be ringwise and not afraid of sudden noises; and lastly he should be something of a show-off. If any of these components are missing, then it is up to you to determine the animal's genuine merits as he appears before you on the day, under those conditions.

Good vs. Mediocre Quality

It is far easier to judge a class of good quality dogs than one containing poor quality. The principal reason for this is that you have many positive elements to work with. You will be satisfied with the dogs that are in the ring and know that your decision is sustainable. You may feel in a bit of a quandry in not knowing which way to turn, having to choose between several really top notch dogs and wishing you could place them all. If you gather your wits about you, however, you will be able to satisfy not only yourself but also all those who are watching. At the Philadelphia show one year, Ramona van Court Jones judged a breed containing several top quality dogs with a finesse that could serve as a model for correct judging. She examined each dog in the Best of Breed Class thoroughly and in narrowing her choice down to two dogs, went back and completely re-evaluated each dog, particle by particle not missing any aspect. The ringside, which was crowded with interested dog people, could clearly see and understand her thinking process. While they did not have the advantage of actually placing their hands on the dogs, they could assess the animals along with her. When she had made her decision everyone watching knew that whether they agreed or not, it was a just and honest appraisal based on a superlative job of judging.

As long as you are able to concentrate fully on the task before you, divesting yourself of emotionalism and other outside factors, you will derive a great deal of personal satisfaction and pleasure from drawing on all the knowledge you have stored within you. Don't ever be afraid of rising up to meet this challenge.

But what about another challenge—that of having to place dogs you really are not too crazy about? How do you handle situations of this sort?

When you are confronted with a class of mediocre dogs having enough merit that you cannot withhold riboons, you will find yourself facing a diametrically opposite problem to that facing you when you are choosing from fairly decent animals. This has to be the most difficult task in judging because you cannot please anyone and most definitely not yourself. You will not be content as you have to measure the various minute plus points versus the overwhelming minuses. If you are not careful, you may find yourself falling deeper and deeper into a trap of getting lost and completely yielding all your concentration powers as you fluctuate between the dogs.

Two of the past masters of this trade had some thoughts on how to judge a class of inferior specimens: Alva Rosenberg—"If they have sufficient merit not to withhold the ribbons, look at them with this idea in mind—which one would you put to sleep first? Second? Third? etc. The remaining four dogs will be your placements!" Percy Roberts—"Look at them as though you are buying them—whether it be as pets or show dogs—as the ones you'll pay the most for are still the four placements!"

Withholding Awards

Most judges hate to withhold ribbons. They may be unsure of themselves, wish to avoid conflicts with exhibitors and do not want to be placed in any possibly embarrassing positions. As more judges gather the courage to withhold in those situations where this is warranted, then these objections should go by the wayside.

If you have a dog that lacks in breed type, you will want to withhold. Otherwise, giving the animal a ribbon it does not deserve, you are encouraging the breeding and showing of fourth-rate specimens.

You may withhold any ribbon from any dog at any time going from first through fourth in the puppy class on up to best in show, and it is solely your decision as to whether you wish to invoke this authority. If you should find yourself in a position where you feel the necessity to withhold, you should do so at the beginning and not wait until the end. In otherwords, do not give out blue ribbons all the way through the classes and then withhold Winners, or give out Winners with points and then withhold Best of Breed. Obviously the exhibitors will find difficulty in following the rationalization of your decision. If you felt the animal was good enough for the blue, why not the purple? And if the dog merited the points in the classes, why not the breed? So, you need to be cautious and avoid coming across as an exhibitionist.

When you withhold state your reasons calmly and kindly to the exhibitor. Do not get into an argument or engage in a debate. Mark your judge's book in the box opposite the armband number the placement withheld and your reason, usually "lack of merit," together with the ribbon you did award, if any.

It is sometimes necessary to be extra courteous when dealing with a complete novice who knows nothing about dog shows. Mrs. Maynard K. Drury shows feeling when she says to beginners, "There are two different kinds of dogs. There are pet dogs and there are show dogs. One is just as nice as the other and really maybe someone told you this is a show dog, but it actually isn't a show dog. You should really take it home and love it."

Excusing Dogs

All judges, at one time or another, find themselves faced with the prospect of having to excuse a dog from the ring. The most common reasons for excusing are lameness and viciousness.

If you notice that a dog is lame, recheck your findings. Be sure he is not hitching or hopping over uneven terrain. Do not be rough if you examine the troubled area. A lame dog should be excused without further delay. Tell the exhibitor that you have to excuse the dog, mark your book opposite the respective number "excused-lame" and continue judging the remaining dogs. Lameness can come on at any time from the class to the breed, into the group and even best in show. It does not matter that you have previously judged and put up the dog. If he suddenly comes up lame he must be excused.

Viciousness is a general term used to describe an animal that tries to bite a judge or is overly aggressive with other dogs, exhibitors or handlers. Always keep your eye out for the angry dog and be sure the exhibitor has a firm hold on him. If upon individually examining the dog, it snaps at you, don't wait for your skin to be broken or believe the exhibitor who says that Fido was only playing. Excuse the dog at once, marking the book "excused—tried to bite me." Caution: viciousness is a disqualification in some standards.

You may excuse any dog that you cannot examine to your satisfaction. Shyness, lack of cooperation by the exhibitor and inability to control an animal are reasons to consider.

A vague area for excusing lies with the possible existence of foreign substance. Hair spray, powder and other cosmetics can generally be detected by feeling or smelling. If its presence is overly obvious, such as when the animal shakes powder flies or your hands turn color after individually examing the dog, you should excuse the animal and mark your book: "excused—foreign substance." Do not disqualify

150

nor let the dog temporarily out of the ring to have the substance removed. He should be totally excused from competition for that day.

Disqualifying

There are several disqualifying factors that judges must consider. Some are breed disqualifications and others are general disqualifications applicable to all breeds. You must be constantly on the alert as to possible situations where such action would be warranted.

General disqualifications are the easiest to recall. Monorchidism and cryptorchidism in males and spaying in bitches are reasons for disqualifying, as are blindness, deafness and artificial changes not approved by breed standard. If you find any of these conditions present, you must disqualify the animal and mark your book "disqualified" with the reason. Caution: it is very difficult to determine by touch if a bitch has been spayed, as well as some surgical alterations.

Disqualification under breed standard is another aspect of judging that needs to be clearly understood and remembered. You need to make mental note of any particular disqualifying features that are listed in the standard. If you are unsure, then stop your examining and recheck the standard which you will have opened on the judge's table. Physical characteristics are readily determined and you have to be conscientious enough to make such decisions. If the dog warrants it, tell the exhibitor that you are disqualifying, state the reason why and mark your book.

Disqualifying on height and weight can be another matter altogether. Many judges do not like to engage in actual measuring or weighing, usually for one or all of the following reasons:

1) Unsure of process.

2) Different dogs can render different results on different days depending if they are mentally up or down, in or out of weight.

3) Rulings are quickly and easily overturned on appeals.

4) Belief that animals out by fractions should not be so severely penalized.

These judges prefer to make their determinations based on eye and mental reasonings. If an animal is too big or too heavy, they will ignore it. Otherwise, they will assess the overall merits and make their judgments taking all factors under consideration.

Nonetheless, in accordance with present rules, you must weigh or measure any animal that you even remotely suspect as falling even a

151

minute fraction of an inch or an ounce outside of the breed standard specifications.

How to Weigh

The necessity to weigh actually comprises two categories: disqualification under breed standard and excusing for being in the wrong class if split by weight divisions. Either way weighing is not done very often. If you are in a position where you need to use the scales, here are some hints:

1) Advise the exhibitor that you are going to weigh his dog.
2) Ask the steward to contact the Superintendent for the scale.
3) When the scale arrives, place it on an even, sturdy surface. Set it at zero and check to see that it is working properly.
4) Ask the exhibitor to center the dog on the scale. Check to be sure all four feet are on.
5) Weigh the animal as expeditiously as possible.
6) If he weighs out, tell the exhibitor and mark your book. An excused dog entered in the wrong weight division cannot be rejudged that day.
7) If he weighs in, continue judging and evaluate the dog without prejudice one way or another.

It is not uncommon for the scale not to work. Judges have been known to fudge the rudimentary process and weigh all animals in. The best procedure, however, is to advise the exhibitors that the scale is not functioning correctly. Find out if another one is easily attainable. If not, judge according to your eye and make note in your judge's book that the scale did not work.

If any problems occur, seek the assistance of the AKC Field Representative and let common sense guide you.

Measuring

Height measurements are disqualifications for twenty-six breeds, ranging from the Toy Poodle to the Great Dane. Some breeds have different disqualifying figures for each sex. It behooves all judges of measurable breeds to be aware of exact measurements, develop an eye for size and thoroughly acquaint themselves with the correct process.

All photos illustrating wicket use on these pages were taken by John Ashbey.

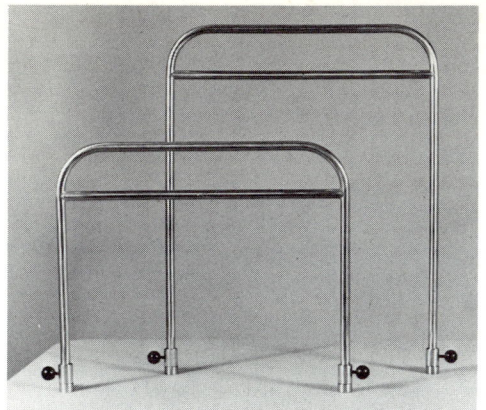

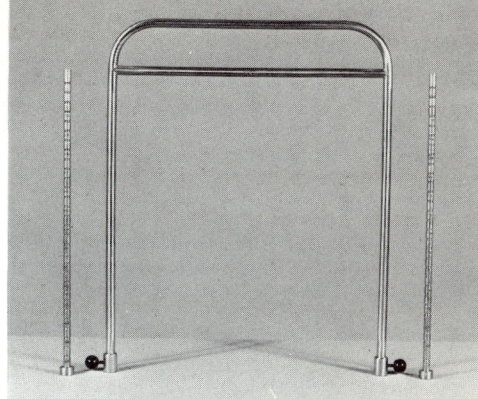

There are two adjustable wickets: the smaller one for heights from 10 to 17 inches and the larger for measurements of 17 to 30 inches.

Both wickets are adjustable by moving the legs with a turn of the black knobs.

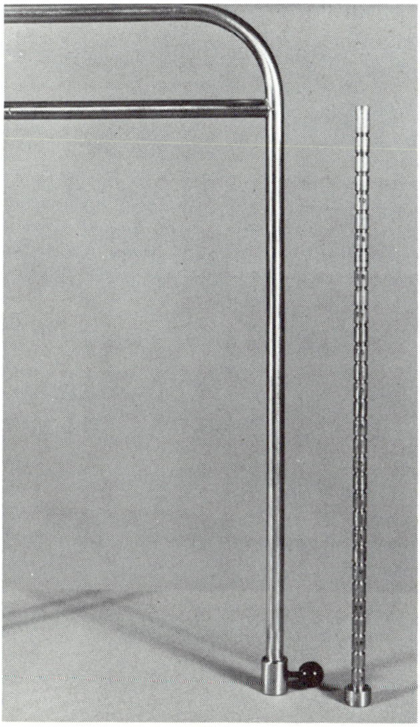

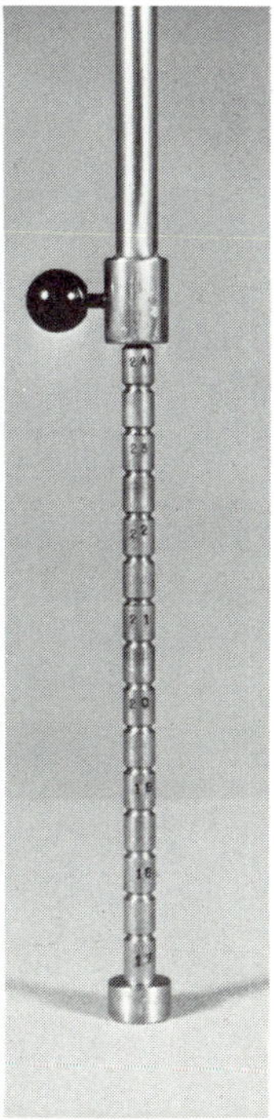

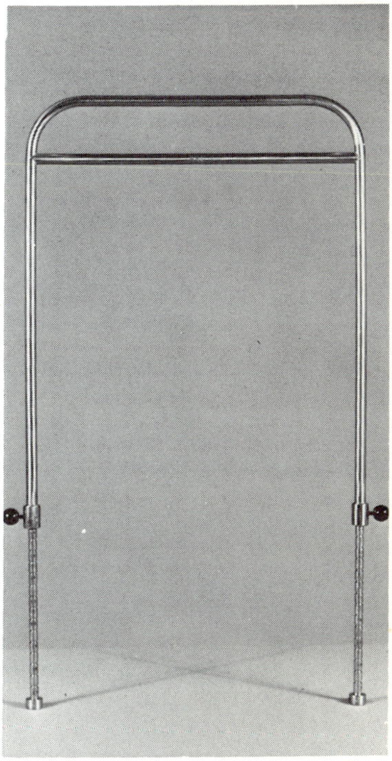

Left: the large wicket showing the calibration from 17 to 30 inches. Center: wicket set for 24½ inches. Right: both legs must be set to the correct measurement.

Before starting to measure be sure the dog is posed as you want him.

Caution: Be sure the dog is not stretched out to make him lower.

Nor pulled up to make him higher.

Place your fingertips on the highest point of the dog's shoulders.

A back view showing the withers

With your other hand, bring the wicket around to the animal's backside holding the wicket in the center of the top crossbar.

Bring the wicket over the rear.

Along the loin

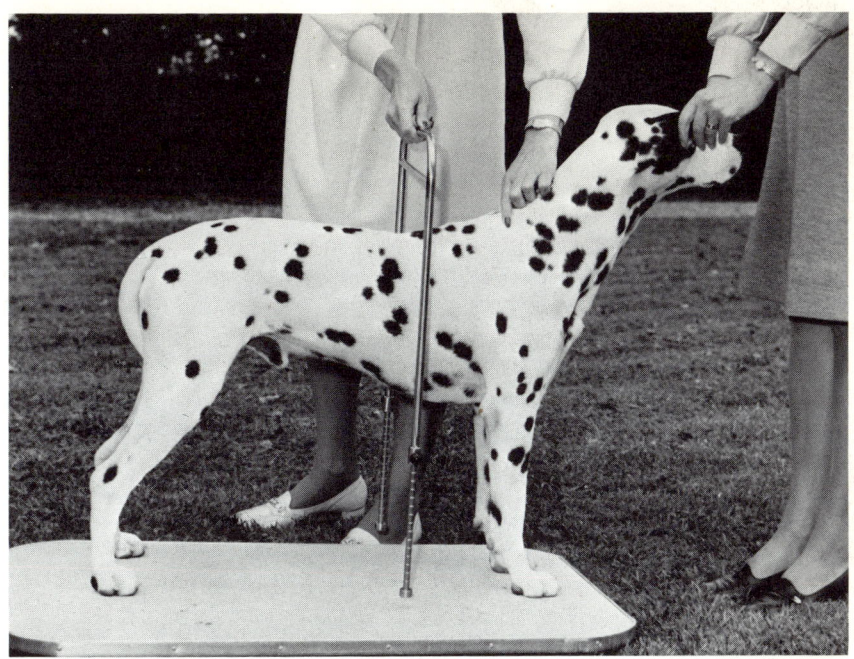

Over the ribs

And let it rest on either the animal or floor surface.

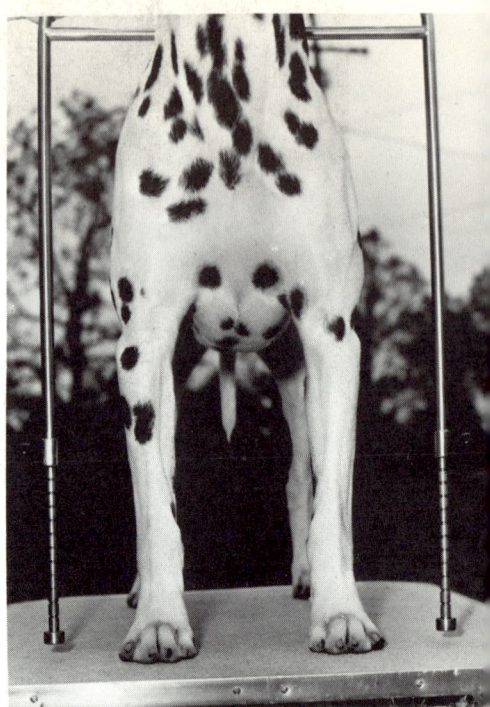

When dog measures "in" on maximum height, both feet rest on table.

If dog measures "out" on maximum height, both feet will not touch surface.

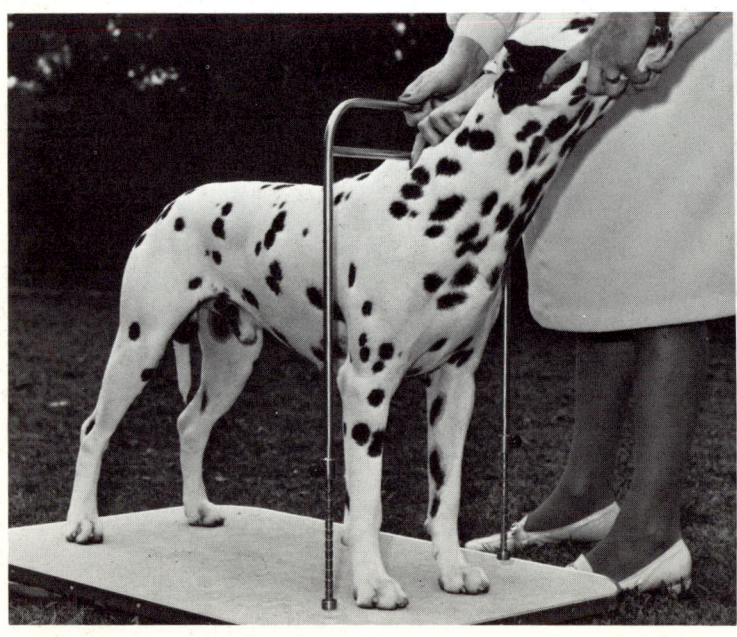

Overall view of dog measuring "out" on maximum height

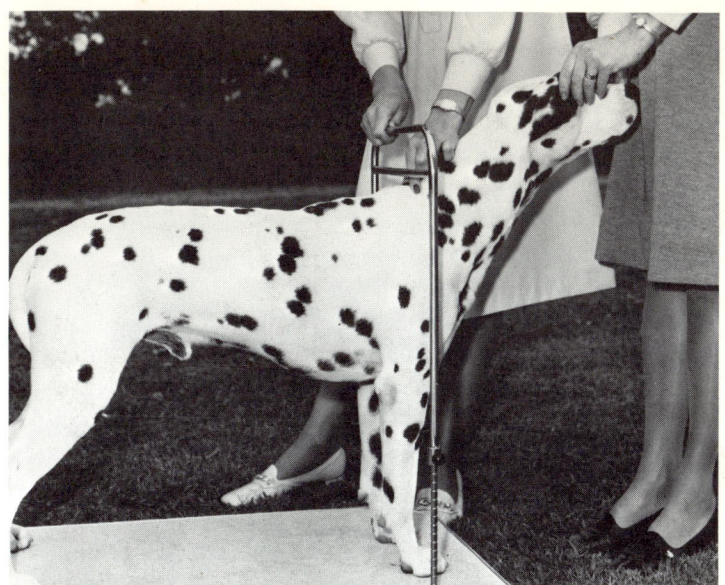

If a dog is too small, the wicket's crossbar will not touch the highest point of the animal's shoulders and he will measure out on minimum disqualifications.

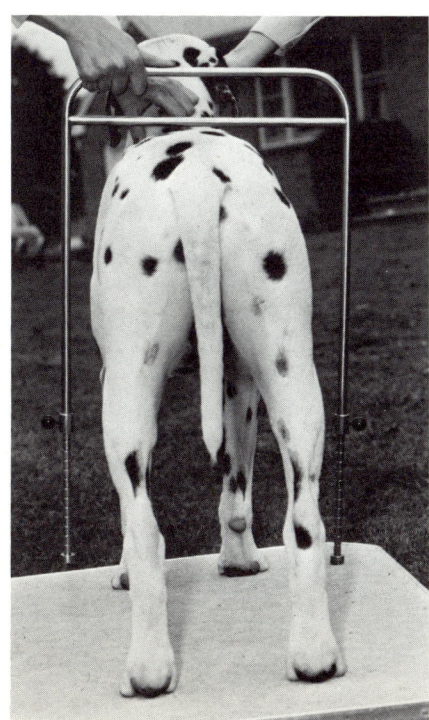

The crossbar should not be held on its corner which gives a tilted measurement instead of an even one.

Nor should dog stand too close to table's edge making the wicket's foot come off the surface.

There are two wickets: one for the larger breeds and the other for the smaller. The particular wicket that you use in the ring is determined by the breed. Here is a simple step-by-step procedure to assist you in calling for a wicket measurement:

1) After appraising the height with your eye and deciding that you must measure, tell the exhibitor that you are going to do so.

2) Ask your steward to procure the proper wicket from the superintendent or show secretary.

3) While you are waiting, ascertain if the exhibitor is familiar with the measuring procedure. If not, tell him why you want to measure his dog, how you are going to do it and what you expect of him.

4) When the wicket comes, check and set it for the correct size measurement.

5) Instruct the exhibitor as to where and how you want the animal to stand.

    a) Breeds that are normally examined on the table must be measured on the table.

    b) A dog measured outdoors on grass must stand on a table top or wide board placed on a level area of the ring. The superintendent or show secretary will provide this.

6) Be sure the dog, physically set up by the exhibitor and not the judge, is standing exactly as you want him—in a normal pose.

    a) Head must be held in typical position, neither drawn up, down nor pulled out, any of which may significantly alter height measurement.

    b) Front legs set evenly under the dog's shoulder, not forward or backward of the shoulder line.

    c) Rear legs positioned properly, neither drawn too far back nor inwards.

7) Tell the exhibitor where you want him to be. Instruct him to stand back away from his animal either to the front or upper righthand side. He may keep a hand beneath the dog's head holding it in correct position while comforting the animal.

8) If you have any problems with any of the above, stop. Do not proceed any further. Give your instructions again until the dog is posing exactly as you want it and not as its exhibitor desires. If you still have a problem, excuse the dog and mark in the judge's book that you were unable to get an honest measurement due to lack of cooperation.

9) Assuming that all is in order, stand on the dog's left side and feel with your left hand (if you are left-handed reverse sides and

hands) for the highest point of the animal's shoulders. If the dog is long-coated, separate the hair so that you can rest the wicket directly upon the skin.

10) With your right hand and in one quick unstopping motion bring the wicket over the dog's rear and place the center of the crossbar on this highest point of the shoulders, the withers. Caution: watch for quick movement by the dog as he feels the weight of the wicket rest on his withers.

11) In maximum qualifications a dog measuring too high will leave one or both of the wicket's feet in the air, not resting on the ground or table, which measures him out. If the wicket totally rests on the ground or table he measures in.

12) In minimum qualifications if the dog is too short, the wicket will rest on the ground or table rather than the withers, measuring it out. If the wicket rests on the animal, with neither foot touching the ground or table, he measures in.

If you had any problems, measure the dog again but don't keep on re-measuring as if you are determined to disqualify or make a point. If the animal measures out, tell the exhibitor that you are disqualifying and mark your book "disqualified-measured out" opposite its number. If the dog measured in, mark the book "measured in" and continue judging without prejudice.

Measuring is not as difficult or as time consuming as it seems to be once you are sure of your procedure. If you have any questions, ask the AKC Representative to demonstrate the wicket, prior to judging.

If your decision to disqualify is later reversed on appeal, do not be disheartened. There are many reasons for reversals which have absolutely nothing to do with your procedure as long as you followed an outline similar to the above with confidence in performance and comprehension in reason. Some hints:

a) Set the wicket at the correct figure.

b) Be sure the animal is positioned to meet your specifications and that the exhibitor's hands are only holding the dog steady and not trying to quickly shift position.

c) Bring the wicket up, over and down in one smooth motion.

d) Make your decision expeditiously without wavering.

e) Don't get into any arguments.

Personality Judgments

Having come this far, you know that your physical actions in the ring have to be second nature while totally concentrating on your mental powers. But there is a third factor that you should keep in the back of your mind without seeming to do so: namely, conveying a proper personality while not letting emotional desire interfere with sound judgment.

Earlier chapters discussed judicial bearing and appropriate image, but they did not cover how you should conduct yourself as a person during different situations that may arise. These situations may be as diverse as being confronted with someone who got up on the wrong side of bed that morning to a young child showing his much beloved pet. The way in which you conduct yourself in the ring has a direct bearing on how well you come across as a respected arbitrator.

While you are judging it is necessary to keep your intuition tuned to the attitude of exhibitors. If you sense that someone is having a bad day or has a chip on his shoulder, go out of your way to pay a little extra attention to his dog. Do not put the dog up unless he merits the win, yet be extra sure as to why you are putting it down. This person is very likely to be the one who will come up to you afterwards demanding an explanation. If you thoroughly and carefully assessed his dog, he cannot honestly feel he was ignored even though he still may not agree with your decision.

Another happenstance to be prepared for is possible comment made by an overeager exhibitor while his dog is being individually examined. The comment may concern the dog's previous wins, needed wins or disparaging remarks about the competition. There are three courses of action you can follow: report the person for a show committee hearing as trying to influence the judge; totally ignore the dog and leave it out of the ribbons as a way of teaching the exhibitor a lesson; or respond, "I'm not interested," and go about your judging as if you did not hear anything at all, placing the dog or not as the quality warrants. Most judges feel that calling for a hearing is a little overbearing in this particular situation and that to ignore the dog is to penalize it for its exhibitor's stupidity. The third course of action would be the best one. You may want to go a step further, however, and make note of the transgression in the judge's book for all to see.

Sometimes a little humor can help to break a tense situation. If you are having trouble getting the kind of response you want out of the animals, have a short quip ready to get the exhibitors to loosen their hold on the dogs. When everyone is relaxed, the dogs will perform better and appear more natural.

The noted all-breed judge, James W. Trullinger, has a favorite story concerning the inadvertent use of humor. A few years ago he was judging smooth-coat Chihuahuas at a southern show when he immediately sensed that one of the dogs was uptight. This dog was shown by an obvious novice exhibitor. As Mr. Trullinger was going over the dog on the table, he asked the owner to show him the animal's teeth. The exhibitor, who was later believed to be either a dentist or a throat doctor, looked down at his pet and said out loud, "Say Ah!"

Humor cannot help in all situations, however, and sometimes you have to keep your defenses up to prevent your self-esteem from being undermined. The insecure judge can waver when someone tells him that he did a lousy job or questions his selections outright, or even overhears derogatory comments made outside the ring. These remarks could be planted with the idea of swaying the judge or may be made by innocuous outsiders. Regardless of which applies, you should be aware and not let anyone's comments shake you to such a degree that you lose your self-confidence.

Another aspect to be aware of concerns human emotionalism and the part it may play in your judgments. For example, everyone loves small kids, sympathizes with the handicapped and sick and knows that the elderly represent one's own future. Nevertheless, these are not reasons to place dogs. You may want to go out of the way to be a little more explicit in your instructions and patient with misunderstandings that might occur. This is perfectly understandable. But if you find yourself being moved by tearfilled, pleading eyes, you must step back, divorce yourself from emotional feelings and reinstate the fact that you are in the ring to judge dogs and only dogs.

The desire to make or break a king is often attributed to emotionalism. There are some judges who like to put down top winners, often to inferior specimens, just to send a quiver through the crowd. They know that their names will be bandied about, but do not realize that they are scoffed at with little value attached to their judgments.

On the diametric side of the fence is the inability by some to honestly evaluate top-winning, well-advertised dogs not shown with their regular handlers. Somehow there is a tendency to associate a dog with a face rather than its overall quality. Good dogs may be defeated because judges are unsure of themselves and afraid of taking a chance on the outsider, who was an insider when campaigned with a particular handler.

10

Judging Pitfalls

$\mathbf{M}$ANY OF THE PROBLEMS in judging are brought upon by the judges themselves. These occurrences may be carefully contrived, unconsciously developed or simply due to a lack of knowledge or experience. It is necessary for all judges to be aware of the existence of snares and know how to prevent entrapment.

Flaws

A few judging faults have been previously mentioned. There are others, however, that should be recognized and cautiously avoided.

One is the failure to judge the dogs as they appear on the day, under those conditions and against that competition. Alongside this flaw comes adherence to precedent where a judge is unable to put down a dog that he had previously favored with a win even though there are better animals in the ring. Every show is a new show, and each dog should be judged as if it were for the first time, regardless of past encounters.

Not paying attention falls on the shoulders of those who spend more time admiring the countryside or passing ringsiders than the dogs in the ring.

Getting lost is like quicksand; it won't loosen its grip until you are drawn in over the brim. Advice given by many experienced judges includes: "Don't fiddle around. If you're confused, don't hesitate. Do something. Do anything. If you make a mistake, make it fast. Your first hunch is usually the correct one so fall back on it."

Never judge by fear. Do not be afraid to put up the better quality newcomer or unknown over a top-rated, heavily advertised dog. It is your opinion and not the ratings, advertisements or others that should be rendered on that day.

Do not allow yourself to be intimidated by any exhibitor. Ignore harsh stares, toothy smiles and wandering eyes.

Prejudices against race, color, creed and sex are acknowledged by all. But what about biases directed towards specific breeds? One should not lean in favor of a particular breed, color, pattern or coat length. All dogs at the breed, group and best in show level should be adjudicated equally. Long-haired dogs should be impartially assessed with their short-haired counterparts. If movement or structure development is a paramount consideration, do not penalize the shorter-coated animals whose faults are glaringly evident over those with concealing long hair.

Most judges would like to become better known as this leads to more assignments which makes it easier for expanding to additional breeds. It is wrong, however, to put up a dog merely because the win is likely to be heavily advertised by an owner who is known to spend a substantial amount of money promoting his animal. Similarly, it is equally in error to award a ribbon to an owner with known show contacts for the principal purpose of obtaining assignments or to trade assignments for wins with other showing judges.

Out of the ring and away from shows for a long period can lead to rustiness. Keep your hand in and your mind tuned by attending shows as an observer.

If you feel that you can no longer handle the task of properly adjudicating dogs, step aside. Nothing is worse than seeing a great judge lose his self-confidence and ability.

Subterfuges

When judging dogs, you want to be able to see the animals at their best—clean, properly conditioned and groomed, alert and well-behaved. It is only natural for the exhibitor also to want to show you his dog at its optimum by trying to hide faults while making the most of the animal's good points. Every judge needs to recognize, accept and expect to see both sides of the coin.

Peter B. Thomson, an all-breed judge with more than fifty years experience both here and abroad, aptly described the artful practice of presenting a dog's best features when he said,

"I believe that anything which is not direct faking and which is allowable in relation to the relevant kennel club's rules and to the standards, is quite OK. I think a handler, exhibitor or breeder is perfectly at liberty to try to outwit the judge and that it is the judge's job to try to find out if an attempt is made to fool him. Whether this is by the method of preparation, handling or allowable trimming; by moving quickly, moving slowly; loose lead, tight lead or whichever way they try to do it, it is all perfectly legitimate and I think it is up to the judge to find it . . . Anything goes as long as it is not illegal, such as dyeing . . . After all, the art of showing is to present the exhibit to the best possible advantage."

By acknowledging the existence of subterfuges, you will be better equipped to take all points under consideration. Delving deeper into what you may see, you will get a clearer understanding of exactly what exists, which in turn enables you to weigh correctly the animal's merits. Don't be afraid to ask the exhibitor to present the dog as you want him presented. An animal being moved too fast should be regaited at a slower speed. Similarly if the dog is strung up tightly, ask for a loose lead. Have the dog stand naturally without being stacked or maneuvered. All of these are methods under your jurisdiction which will counter good handling that is designed to present the dog's finer aspects while covering up his faults.

You need carefully to study handling techniques and subterfuges to decipher the difference between what appears and what actually exists under the disguise of masterful illusions. Put what you learn to use in the ring as you totally and carefully evaluate the animals that come before you.

One judging flaw to avoid is putting up a dog just because you had previously favored it with a win. Always remember that each show is a new event with different competition and conditions. *Foster—GAZETTE, American Kennel Club*

11

Protests in the Ring

RECOURSE EXISTS within the bounds of AKC rules for questioning by persons, other than the judge, about possible infractions of rules and breed eligibilities. This recourse, known as the right to protest, may be lodged in one of the following ways:

Verbal——A verbal protest can only be made by an exhibitor in the ring against another competing dog in that class, before the judge has marked his book. Made directly to the judge, the protester must clearly state the dog's number and the reason for protest. Verbal protests specifically cover either general or breed disqualifications, lameness, colorations or ineligibility under class requirements.

The judge examines the dog in question for the alleged condition, making a determination as to whether or not the protest is valid. If the protest is sustained and the reason a disqualification, the dog is disqualified and the judge marks his book accordingly. If the reason leads to excusing the dog or withholding of ribbons, then this is done with proper book markings.

If the judge does not find justifiable cause for the protest, he makes note of his findings in his book and proceeds without prejudice against any of the parties involved.

Written——A written protest can be lodged by any exhibitor or member of a member club of the AKC against any dog entered in a specific show. Clearly stating the purpose and dog involved, the protest must be made in writing to the secretary of the show giving club, with a deposit of $5. If the protest is such that an immediate determination is necessary, it should be filed before the end of the show and action will be taken at once. Otherwise, seven days from the end of the event are allotted for filing.

Written protests that must be dealt with on the day cover those areas dealing with an animal's physical condition and eligibility. The bench show committee appoints a protest committee, comprised of club members, recognized authorities and/or judges, to examine the dog in question. This committee reports its findings and the protest is either sustained or denied. If sustained, any wins that the animal may have acquired during the day will be nullified. An appeal procedure to the AKC exists for aggrieved parties which could reverse the findings.

The judge needs only to concern himself with verbal protests that are lodged in his ring. Written protests are not under his jurisdiction unless upon completion of his assignments he is requested to serve on a protest committee.

Hearings

A bench show committee hearing is to some extent a quasi-judicial proceeding. The committee members act as judge, jury and prosecutor hearing all facts and rendering disciplinary determinations. They have the right to suspend any person from all AKC privileges for conduct prejudicial to the best interests of pure-bred dogs, dog shows, obedience trials or the AKC, which occurred in connection with or during the progress of its show or obedience trial.

Dog show judges may become involved in hearings when they apprise a show chairman of any scenes or altercations they have witnessed and believe are detrimental to the best interests of the sport. Examples of misbehavior directly affecting the judge include refusal to accept a ribbon or throwing the same on the ground, disregard for ring instructions, improper suggestions or requests, abusive or foul language and inhumane treatment of a dog.

If, while judging, you are subjected to any of the above and feel that disciplinary proceedings should be taken against an individual, ask your steward to call for the show chairman. Relate to him exactly what you witnessed and heard and let him take the matter from there. Chances are the AKC representative will also have suggestions as to proper recourse.

On being called into a hearing as a witness, tell your story concisely, without emotionalism and then remove yourself from the picture. The decision as to whether any punitive action is required rests solely with the bench show committee. A report of its findings is filed with the AKC. If suspension is recommended, the length of time for such suspension is determined by the AKC upon receipt of all facts involved, subsequent appeals and reinstatement requests.

You should not stand in awe of good handling techniques.
Cummin—GAZETTE, American Kennel Club

12

Officials

W<small>HEN SOMETHING IS AMISS</small>, to whom do you look for assistance? Who is responsible for the over-all show? What is the relationship of the judge to the AKC field representative? superintendent/show secretary/show chairman?

Before you can begin to understand the answers to these questions, it is necessary to picture in your mind the dog show concept: an event benefiting pure-bred dogs sponsored by individual kennel clubs, following rules and guidelines established by the AKC. Every show is a separate entity unto itself. Clubs are free to do as they please so long as they remain within the basic rules. Shows are the sole responsibility of the clubs. Whatever happens during show hours is under the jurisdiction of the club, specifically its show committee and chairman. The superintendent is merely an agent hired by the club. The field representative is present to observe and give advice. When things go astray, the resources of all three are pooled together, but the ultimate burden of decision rests with the chairman.

Let's take a closer look at the functions of the field representative, superintendent and show chairman in correlation with the judge:

AKC Field Representative

Field reps have two primary responsibilities at a show: to observe judging and be available for assistance as needed.

170

As there is neither enough time nor reps, not all judges are observed. Instead, concentration centers on provisionals, new judges and those applying for additional breeds. At the conclusion of the show, reps file a judge's observation report covering the following areas: ability, appearance, presence, competence, consistency, procedure, control, quality of competition, number of dogs judged, ring conditions, time spent observing and any unusual occurrences. The information on these reports is placed in each respective adjudicator's file.

When watching judges some reps will make a note of any aspects of technique that they feel can be improved. Later, at the completion of the assignment, they will try to talk quietly with the judge involved. Judges are not interrupted during judging for anything other than a gross procedural error that requires immediate correction.

Reps also try to conduct oral interviews of prospective and additional breed judges during show hours. Generally having no set time span, they are wedged in between other chores.

Besides observing and interviewing, a field representative can also be a helpful ally to the officiating judge who finds himself confronted with unusual problems. Dog shows being what they are, anything can and does happen, and it is a wise judge who consults the rep if he has a question. Occasionally with no precedence to fall back on, reps are required to shoot from the hip when they have to give advice as to immediate solutions for uncommon circumstances. Their assistance is always valued, but caution yourself not to stand in their awe, afraid to voice your individual opinion. Always remember that the ring is yours and you, as the judge, are the sole adjudicator so long as you stay within the bounds of AKC rules and regulations.

The rep is also on hand to assist the show chairman in his duties, if requested. He is not, however, to preempt the chairman. The running of the show is not his responsibility. He may make a report of his observations as to the conduct of the show, but he is never to interfere with the actual process.

As the AKC man-on-the scenes he frequently spends his day listening to suggestions, gripes and what have you from all aspects of the fancy. He needs to have a ready answer for just about any conceivable question concerning every facet of the sport; to be patient when asked the same query over and over again; to be a calming influence between agitated parties; and, last but not least, to be aware that he is regarded as representing the AKC in everything he says and does.

171

Superintendent/Show Secretary

The superintendent and his staff are paid by the club to operate the show. As its agent, the superintendent/show secretary takes care of many details, such as mailings, entries, layout, equipment, printing, ribbons, prize money, judges' bags, catalogs, judges' books and the filing of final AKC show reports.

Responsible for keeping an eye on the progress of the show, anticipating delays, ring problems and incidents, he works hand in hand with the show chairman in seeing that the event is operating smoothly and efficiently.

Conscientious superintendents help judges in being sure that their books are correctly marked. Often when transferring markings from the sheets to a catalog, an error may be found. The superintendent will page the respective judge to see if he is still on the grounds, and if so, have him make and initial the necessary amendments. If corrections are not made prior to the filing of the official judges' sheets with the AKC, the errors would be subsequently discovered by the AKC resulting in a letter to the judge requesting clarification and correction.

Upon completion of the show, the superintendent/show secretary must file with the AKC a show report, which, as you can see, covers many aspects concerning judges.

Show Chairman

With the power invested in him by the show giving club and its committee, the show chairman is the supreme authority at his show. He is the person who is entrusted with the ultimate accountability for the success or failure of the event. He has to oversee the workings of the superintendent and stewards, keep track of the progress in all rings, and be conscientious about the overall well-being of spectators, exhibitors, handlers and judges. He must be everywhere at once and always have his finger on the pulse beat of the show.

In his lap falls the final decisions on whether or not any changes need to be made during the show's duration: rings moved, judges prodded, delays allocated, hours extended and schedules changed as conditions warrant. These decisions are usually made after seeking the advice of the superintendent and AKC field rep.

The show chairman is responsible for the judges. He, or the

REPORT OF DOG SHOW OR OBEDIENCE TRIAL

Upon the completion of a dog show or obedience trial the Superintendent or Show Secretary or Trial Secretary is to fill out this form and mail it within four days following the show or trial. It is to be sent to the Executive Secretary of the American Kennel Club, 51 Madison Avenue, New York, N.Y. 10010. Each question should be answered fully. All other records required in the Rules shall be filed with the American Kennel Club (Show Records Dept.) within seven days after a show or trial. 'Filed' means in the office of the American Kennel Club.

Name of Club_____

Location of show (exact location, not just the name of city or town)_____

_____

Date of show_____ Give date and hour when entries closed_____

Number of dogs entered_____ *Recording Fees enclosed $*_____

Did all the judges approved by the American Kennel Club for this show officiate?_____

If "No", name the judges below giving the date on which you or the club received notification of his inability to judge, and stating the reason as reported to you.

Name_____Date Notified_____Reason_____

_____

Name_____Date Notified_____Reason_____

_____

Name_____Date Notified_____Reason_____

_____

In the above instances was American Kennel Club approval obtained for substitute judges?_____

_____

_____

If AKC approval was not obtained for any substitute judge, give below the name and address of the person (s) selected to judge in place of the scheduled judge (s), and the breed (s) judged by him (them).

Name_____ Address_____

Breeds judged_____

Name_____ Address_____

Breeds judged_____

Name_____ Address_____

Breeds judged_____

Were all such persons eligible for approval by the AKC for the breeds judged?_____If "No" list exceptions below and explain on a separate sheet (8½ X 11)_____

_____

_____

Superintendent's/show secretary's report, filed with the AKC after a show, has many questions dealing directly with the judges of the event.

Give name of any judge who arrived at the show late for his assignment _____

Name_____ How Late?_____

Name_____ How Late?_____

Name_____ How Late?_____

Were there any complaints against the judges? If so, state who made them, basis of complaint, and give name of the judge. If you have any information in support of complainant or judge please give details. (Use separate sheet [8½ X 11] if needed)_____

_____

_____

Outline below any unusual occurrences in the judging rings (Obedience rings included). It is very important that such happenings be reported by you in detail. This applies whether the incident was brought to a satisfactory conclusion or not. (Use separate sheet [8½ X 11] if needed).

_____

_____

_____

_____

Give a resume of any occurrences outside the judging rings, but within the show area that you think should be reported to the AKC (Use separate sheet [8½ X 11] if needed)_____

_____

_____

_____

Report on a separate 8½ X 11 sheet a resume of all calls by judges for veterinarians and requests by judges that dogs be measured or weighed.

Report on a separate 8½ X 11 sheet any request made by an owner or handler that his dog be measured or weighed prior to the judging of its breed. Describe how his requests were handled, stating the determination that was made by the measurers or weighers appointed by the Bench Show Committee.

Was the show benched or unbenched?_____

What were the opening and closing hours of the show as published in the premium list?_____

At what time was the judging of the show scheduled to start?_____Obedience Trial?_____

At what time did the judging of the show start?_____Obedience Trial?_____

At what time was the judging of the show completed?_____Obedience Trial?_____

   (A) What provisions, if any, were contained in the premium list in regard to the arrival of dogs and exhibitors at the show after the opening hour?_____

_____

   (B) What provisions, if any, were contained in the premium list in regard to the excusing of dogs and exhibitors prior to the closing hour?_____

_____

Give names and addresses of exhibitors or handlers who did not comply with (A). List the entry numbers of their dogs and excuses given.

_____

_____

_____

Give names and addresses of exhibitors or handlers who removed their dogs without permission prior to the time all dogs were excused_____

_____

_____

If any of the provisions of (A) or (B) were changed by the bench show committee after the show opened, explain the changes and give reasons for the action_____

_____

_____

Give the names of the veterinarians or the veterinarian association listed in the premium list and catalog_____

_____

_____

_____

Give the names of the veterinarians in actual attendance at the show and schedule of coverage_____

_____

_____

_____

If at least one veterinarian was not in attendance during the entire progress of the show (or trial) give *complete* details on a separate sheet (8½ X 11).

Was a suitable "veterinarian headquarters", as described in chapter 13, section 6 provided._____ If the answer is "no" please give a full explanation on a separate 8½ X 11 sheet.

Was this an "examined" show or trial?_____

If "yes" give on a separate 8½ X 11 sheet a complete description of the way in which the matter was handled i. e. **Number of** veterinarians on hand for the inspection of dogs, description of the "enclosure" provided and facilities furnished for **the use of** the veterinarians.

Were any entries as listed in the judges' books and catalog changed at the show?_____

If so, explain_____

_____

_____

Were any entries added to the judges' books and catalog?_____ If so, explain_____

_____

_____

_____

Was an area provided for unentered dogs?_____

Was the place where the show was held satisfactory *in all respects?* Give details and do not hesitate to be frank in your appraisal

_____

_____

_____

Were clean and orderly conditions maintained throughout the show precincts during the show?_____

_____

_____

(SIGNED)_____
Superintendent, Show or Trial Secretary

(SIGNED)_____

(SIGNED)_____

(SIGNED)_____

The signature of *all* superintendents at a show are required.

Attach all report forms completed by Veterinarians.
If an area was furnished by the club for unentered dogs attach all forms completed by owners and handlers.

      If any meetings of the Bench Show or Obedience Trial Committee were called, give full details on a separate sheet (8½ X 11) attach to this report and sign your name. Be sure to list the names of members of the Bench Show or Obedience Trial Committee in attendance, name of person taking notes at meeting, names and addresses of all other persons present. If the purpose of the meeting was to consider a protest against a dog, then in addition to the above information, give the dog's entry number and registered name. Give the time at which the meeting occurred. In your report you must certify that the Bench Show or Obedience Trial Committee was fully informed as to all the provisions of Chapter 20, Sections 2 and 4 and Chapter 24, Section 2 of the "Rules Applying to Registration and Dog Shows."

chairman of the judging committee, if any, makes the initial contacts, works with hospitality to see to those arrangements, connects with the superintendent as to location, layout and ring size, signs all contracts and is ex-officio member of all show committees.

He is the person with whom you, the judge, will have the most contact. If you have any problems or questions, check with him.

This job is not an easy one, nor should it be taken lightly. Chester F. Collier, show chairman for Westminster Kennel Club, an event that surpasses all others in reputation, problems and ambience, gives an excellent insight into a show chairman's obligation in the following interview excerpts on selecting judges:

". . . The most important function of the show chairman is putting together the judging slate because the show will be as good as its slate. He should solicit, from those members of the club who are knowledgeable, suggestions for judges for various breeds. He should then evaluate those names. It is assumed that he is qualified to know good judges from bad judges and be able to ascertain this from observing or talking to people. He should set as criteria honesty first and knowledge second, both very close. The thing above all that he must avoid is cronyism where he selects his friends to judge. If he is an exhibitor or has been an exhibitor, he must put behind him any decisions that judges have made regarding his dogs when weighing who will judge. If a judge, he must avoid what is perhaps the greatest sin of all—the terrible practice of swapping assignments."

On breaking club restrictions for a longer time period or territorial mileage than the thirty-day, two-hundred mile limit set by the AKC:

". . . If a judge breaks the club's restriction, the show chairman has to remove that person from the panel. He doesn't really have any alternative. If he doesn't remove him from the panel, then the rule means nothing the next year."

On the slow or problematical judge:

". . . The show chairman has got to be very tactful. First of all he should determine whether slowness is being caused by an inefficient steward or if there is something external going on around the ring that is making it difficult for dogs to get in and out quickly. But once having determined that the judge himself is falling behind, the chairman should step into the ring during a break and speak with the judge in an unobtrusive way so that neither the spectators nor other exhibitors think that the show chairman is doing anything more than just going in and saying 'Hi. How are you?' It mustn't be evident to anyone other than the judge and the show chairman that there is a problem. The chairman should tactfully point the problem out to the judge, always keeping in mind that the judge is the complete and final arbiter in the ring in all mattters. Many judges, particularly new judges, are not aware of how long they are taking. They are not aware that they are going slow. It is very easy to set into a pattern and not realize that you've done it. So, I think that you can approach the judge and if the judge says that's tough, then it is tough. The show is going to go on at that speed and that's certainly a thing for the show chairman to remember in the future when considering that judge again."

On the officials:

". . . The show chairman has the ultimate responsibility for the show. This is spelled out by the American Kennel Club and the wise chairman will keep in mind and recognize that fact. If something goes wrong at the show, the show giving club is responsible. It will be fined or reprimanded. There is no way for the chairman to say, 'Yes, but the superintendent or rep told me.' That's not sufficient. The show chairman must know the rules, know how to run a show and be confident in his knowledge. He can tactfully deal with a field rep, superintendent or an exhibitor who differs with him. It is not necessary for confrontations and they can and should be avoided. Basically everything that goes on is the responsibility of the show chairman. The AKC rep is there as an advisor. The superintendent is hired by the show-giving club and has the responsibility to carry out the wishes of the club as long as he's not asked to violate the rules and regulations of the American Kennel Club. The bottom of all this is that the responsibility for the show cannot be handed over to anyone else. It is the responsibility of the show chairman, the show committee, the show-giving club."

On the decision making process:

". . . In planning the show, the chairman should consult with his committee. He makes the final decisions, but it would be unwise to not utilize the chairmen of the various committees and get input from all members on any area, letting them participate in all phases from the make-up of the judging slate to parking, rather than just segregating their tasks. Committee members must feel a part of the show and know that they helped to make it work. On the day of the show, the chairman must make decisions alone as they happen; that is why he is the chairman. As he cannot be an intuitive being, knowing all the answers to all things, when faced with a problem on the day of the show to which he doesn't know the answer, he should make use of the superintendent, AKC rep or anybody on his committee who might have the answer."

As a judge, you have an opportunity to experience first-hand the diverse, yet cross-purpose, functions of show officials. When something goes amiss, or a question arises, it is good to know that there are competent and knowledgeable persons present to give advice and assistance. Don't hesitate to call on them.

13

Post-mortem

YOUR ASSIGNMENT IS FINISHED . You have handed out the last ribbon, posed for the final picture and given your signed, marked judge's book to the superintendent. What do you do now? How do you feel? Anticlimatic or riding the crest of euphoria?

For your first few shows you will probably be breathing a sigh of relief. Happy yet sad that your time in the ring is over—you escaped unscathed while appreciating the sense of power and authority that enveloped your consciousness.

As you gain more experience, you will come to terms with the mental process of putting judging in its proper perspective. The more you judge, the more self-confident you become, which in turn leads to better judging.

Staying Around

Do not feel that you must leave the grounds immediately just because your time in the ring is over. Instead you would be wise to stay around, watch other judging and increase your educational exposure.

By remaining at the show you do, of course, subject yourself to the

Sometimes losers are openly indignant and obnoxious.
Duncan—GAZETTE, American Kennel Club

However, the sincere owner would like your honest assessment of his dog and looks to you for guidance.
Harding—GAZETTE, American Kennel Club

possibility of coming across an irate exhibitor. You will soon discover that these encounters are best dealt with by using a little political expertise. Size up the complainant. Does this person seem like a chronic complainer with an axe to grind? If so, nothing you could say would mollify him. Don't waste your time telling him everything that was wrong with his animal. He's not interested in that. His only interest is in deriving a sadistic satisfaction of putting you down. Merely retort to his questions with something like the following and walk away: "I really liked the other dog (dogs) better today."

On the other hand, the exhibitor who comes up to you after judging may truly be someone who is sincerely interested in his animal's merits or lack thereof. If you detect this sincerity, respond likewise. You are doing this person a favor be being tactfully honest in your judgment of his pet.

You do have a problem, however, if your spouse or best friend is predisposed to vocally tearing your decisions apart. Constructive criticism has its time and place, but the show grounds do not serve that purpose. It is better to wait until returning home to engage in discussions with your trusted ally.

Never justify poor or political decisions by blatantly pulling apart the dogs you did not put up, especially to other judges and friends. These remarks have a way of coming back to haunt you. If ever asked why you did not like so and so, turn the questions around and fall back on the positive as opposed to the negative.

One of the best stories concerning the way in which an old-time judge inadvertently handled an irate exhibitor in such a fashion as to leave her speechless is told by William L. Kendrick, who is renowned not only as a respected arbiter but also for his many chronicles of dog shows past.

"There was a toy judge, a judge of all toys, and quite an authority on them. She was stone deaf and I think if you looked right at her, she could understand a little of what you said. It was an outdoor show and our judging tables were back to back. She (this lady long since dead) had a rather good size entry of Maltese. When she had concluded her judging, a rather comely looking, modishly dressed lady came in and said, 'Mrs. Blank, what took place in this ring today was a disgrace to you, a disgrace to Maltese and a disgrace to the show giving club. I have every intention of taking this up with the American Kennel Club.' Whereupon Mrs. Blank said, 'Just a minute, honey,' as she reached into her bag, a large shopping bag, bringing out a horn which she puts to her ear. The girl repeats this diatribe word for word. Whereupon Mrs. Blank's face lights up like a Christmas tree and she says, 'Don't thank me, honey. Thank the little dog!' ''

Written or Oral Critiques

Some specialty clubs ask their judges to give written critiques for their breed magazine or oral critiques at the club dinner following the show. How you handle either one depends a great deal on your particular feelings about critiques: Is a critique suppose to be a blow by blow description of each and every dog in the class or every animal that receives a ribbon? Or, should your analysis cover the basic points of what you found to be good and bad in the over-all quality of the dogs you judged that day?

If you subscribe to the former school of thought, your critiques will be in depth and may reveal considerably more than the owners wished. Therefore, keeping this thought in mind, your criticism of individual dogs should follow a set pattern with all animals receiving like treatment. If you are judging a large entried specialty show, you may wish to use a tape recorder while in the ring. If this is your desire, at the end of each class after you mark your book and hand out the ribbons and trophies, have the dogs remain beside their respective placings and take your portable recorder out into the middle of the ring. Face the dogs and speak quietly and concisely into the machine. After the assignment is finished, you can transcribe the tape into written words and edit your critique from these notes. While this is the best way to keep every dog straight and remember all the features, you must be cautious and not take too much time recording.

General critiques are prescribed by many as the best system. Advocates maintain that the owners do not really want everyone to know their animals' specific faults. It is also conceivable for different judges to weigh opposing aspects with opposite results. And critiques, at their very best, fail accurately to convey the mental thought process used in evaluating the dogs individually and collectively. A broad statement of the status of the breed at the time, problems to be aware of and thoughts on the future will usually suffice as a general written or oral critique.

Whatever policy you adopt, it is necessary to always keep in mind that the positive as opposed to the negative should be emphasized. It is far easier to get a point across by gently intermingling adverse

182

comments with affirmative statements. The idea will come through without offending the reader or listener.

Second Thoughts

It is not sacrilege for a judge to admit that occasionally he has second thoughts. Thoughts may vary from not having seen something he should have in a particular dog, failing to totally evaluate the animals in the ring, the inability to divorce oneself from outside circumstances or having just a plain bad day. Anything is possible and it is necessary for all persons involved to understand an occasional lapse in performance.

Second thoughts should not be dismissed, but reckoned with and you needn't penalize yourself so long as you comprehend that to self-question is human nature. It is when you continuously doubt your decisions that you need to stop and seriously consider whether you have undermined your ability with a lack of confidence. If this has happened, consider stepping aside entirely or for a short breather to enable you to rebuild your confidence.

Use second thoughts for self-education, deciding whether they were merely figments of your imagination or based on solid reasoning. The best way to study this is mentally to rejudge the dogs in question or avail yourself of the possible opportunity to see the dogs together at a different show, under another judge, when you are just a spectator and re-evaluate them from outside the ring. Many times your original findings will stand and you will come to terms with the indecisiveness that followed. If the findings are not sustained, you will have learned from the process by enabling yourself to see or think what you might have missed in the previous encounter with a promise to avoid that trap in the future.

14

The Mail Bag

IF YOU THOUGHT that your dealings with the mailman ended with pre-show contacts, you will soon discover that you're not through yet. There are many instances where post-show correspondence is necessary and thank you letters abound. It is good manners to say thank you when someone has been particularly kind. Many clubs go out of their way to see to it that their judges are comfortable and well looked after. Finding something cool to drink, fruit, cheese, crackers or even flowers in one's room is evidence that someone went out of his way to make you comfortable. Special treats and efforts deserve a thank you note to the person responsible.

Some clubs give show or location mementos to their judges. These gifts are often in addition to payment for services rendered and should be appropriately acknowledged after the show to the chairman in writing.

Photographs received after the show of yourself with a winning dog and its exhibitor should also be acknowledged. But don't send a thank you for pictures received just prior to a show which were obviously sent with the intent to prejudice your decision.

Gifts

Judges should not accept gifts from exhibitors before or after a show. Presents are sent for the principal purpose of swaying opinion in favor of particular dogs. A gift is merely a substitute for a monetary bribe and should be regarded as such. If the sender's name appears on the outside of the box, you can readily determine that the contents do not contain something you ordered and refuse to accept the same. The cost of returning the item is then borne by the original sender. If you have already opened a package and discovered that it represented a gift, just rewrap and return it.

Christmas gifts, birthdays and other special occasions when one usually receives gifts should be treated in the same manner. A rule of thumb to follow is that if the gift-giver is a friend with whom you have always exchanged presents, you do not have to stop the exchange just because you are now a judge. However, if you are suddenly the recipient of a gift from someone who is not a close friend, you can correctly assume that your judging status is the cause of the present and not friendship. Immediately return this present, unopened if possible.

An exception to all the above is the innocent present of flowers or some other innocuous item sometimes sent by the novice exhibitor who just finished his first champion and wants to share his joy with you for having given his animal the final points. In cases like this you need to carefully weigh in your mind the intention of the present.

Outright bribes, whether monetary, gifts, trips or the like should never be condoned.

Poison Pen Letters

At sometime or other during your judging career you are bound to receive a poison pen letter or two. The initial one is always a shock, but as time wears on you soon shrug your shoulders. If the letters are signed, make a copy for your files and send the original to the AKC. Also follow this procedure with any other correspondence that is sent with the intent to influence your decision making process.

Unsigned papers have little value as the sender's name cannot be easily traced. If the information contained therein is pertinent, copy it and forward the original to the AKC. If not, destroy the letter and put the matter out of your mind.

Letters to the AKC

Correspondence received by the AKC includes not only documents you sent to them, but also letters they may have received about you.

Generally, if the statements are detrimental or accusatory in nature regarding a judge, the AKC will contact the writer and request clarification or further supporting documents. If you find yourself embroiled in an inquiry, tell your facts straight and honestly. Request a copy of the accuser's statement and the right to confront and defend yourself from false remarks that may end up in your AKC file. Keep photocopies of all correspondence in the matter and if you feel that you have been maligned without cause, consult an attorney.

Judges should always be aware of motives behind gift-giving and back-slapping. *Foster—GAZETTE, American Kennel Club*

15

Foreign Assignments

IT IS A PLEASURE to judge dogs in a foreign country, but it also requires patience, understanding and knowledge. You not only have to cope with possible language difficulties, but also quickly adapt to a different system. Shows, ring procedures, breed standards, grooming and handling techniques may vary. Before going learn as much as possible.

Foreign assignments usually come to you through the recommendations of friends or friends of friends. You may receive a letter of inquiry or a last minute, by American standards, telephone call. In either case, try immediately to gather as much information as possible regarding dog shows in that country and its kennel club requirements. Find out the approximate duration of your stay for the show, possible transportation and lodging reservations to be handled by the host club and other relevant travel tips. If you are to pay your own expenses with reimbursement from the club, request payment in U.S. funds. This way you will not be hurt by the fluctuating exchange rates. Also, checks drawn on a bank with U.S. offices are processed faster by your own bank when deposited.

As soon as the assignment is confirmed, write to the governing kennel club for a copy of its rules and regulations, breed standards and any other information you may need. If the host language is unknown, request English translations, if available. Study this material and if you have any questions, ask either this body or the person who originally contacted you for clarification.

Before leaving home read up on the customs and local color of the country you are visiting, which serves to give you an idea of what to expect. Also be sure to review the U.S. duty law for bringing items back home with you. If you are to be out of the country for less than forty-eight hours, keep in mind that the amount allocated for duty-free purchases is $10. Be sure your passport and visa, if required, are up to date and any required medical procedures are taken.

Some tips on judging abroad: judge by that country's standards; be patient if things seem less professional than you are accustomed to; be prepared to be flexible; always ask for assistance when needed, remembering the adage, "When in Rome, do as the Romans do!"—and return home having left some of your knowledge behind and taken with you some of theirs to the enrichment of all.

Different judging procedures are used in many foreign countries. Before going, thoroughly acquaint yourself with customs and standards. *Foster—GAZETTE, American Kennel Club*

16

Bookkeeping,
the IRS and You

As YOU HAVE SEEN, judging does not begin and end with
a particular event. A judge's life is forever constant as new shows
come in and old ones are past. One important task often overlooked,
or conveniently forgotten, is the necessity of keeping adequate financial records. Good recordkeeping is a must as it helps you to keep
track of all your income and expenses connected with judging and will
serve to satisfy the Internal Revenue Service agent if he takes a
sudden interest in your activities. Whether you judge a few times a
year or many times, you should take the time, when returning home
from a show, to write all financial transactions in a ledger, staple and
file all receipts and keep track of bills that follow.

Ledger

The easiest way to tell where you stand money-wise is by maintaining an on-going, yearly ledger that shows all income and expenses
incurred. This ledger is important to both the hobby judge and the

SAMPLE LEDGER PAGE FOR A PROFESSIONAL JUDGE

	1980	Explanation	Income		Mileage	Air Fare
1						
2						
3						
4						
5						
6	Apr. 16	Roosevelt K.C., Hyde Park, N.Y.				
7	17	fee + expenses	464 92			
8		auto			50 mi	
9		air fare				187
10		parking + tolls				
11		lodging				
12		meals				
13	18	Dry cleaning				
14		Post Office - stamps				
15		B & P Stationary - letter heads				
16	20	Howell Book House				
17	21	Bell Telephone Co.				
18	23	Blue Mountain K.C.	493 85			
19	24	Crestridge, Tenn.				
20		Silver Spur K.C.	493 86			
21		Oakville, Tenn.				
22		Transportation				
23		airport limo				
24		air fare				269
25		car rental				
26		Motels				
27		Meals				
28	27	Dry cleaning				
29	30	Wheaton K.C. Pine Bush, Ill.	305 -			
30		fee + expenses				
31		mileage - auto			378 mi	
32		tolls				
33		Motel				
34		Meals				
35						
36						
37						
38						
39						
40						

	parking, tolls + limo	Other transportation	Motel / Hotel	Meals	Misc'l show exp.	Books + Periodicals	Telephone	Office Expense	
5		6	7	8	9	10	11	12	
									1
									2
									3
									4
									5
					3 —				6
									7
									8
									9
	10 —								10
			35 —						11
				7 50					12
					3 50				13
								15 —	14
								29 35	15
						14 95			16
							34 89		17
					5 —				18
									19
									20
									21
									22
	30 —								23
									24
		153 32							25
			80 —						26
				51 64					27
					3 50				28
									29
									30
									31
	250								32
			26 50						33
				23 25					34
									35
									36
									37
									38
									39
									40

career professional and should be adapted to suit the individual involved. This is a sample ledger entry covering a single show for the hobby judge, who officiates a few times a year and can maintain simplified records in a notebook:

Date	Item	Income	Expenses
2/21/80	Oak Hills Kennel Club	$80.00	
	Mileage—200 mi. at .20		$40.00
	Tolls		1.50
	Motel		22.50
	Meals		16.00

The more active judge, who should keep careful records of income and expenses, will use a multi-columned ledger book. Columns are established for all transportation expenses, lodging, meals and other costs directly related to traveling to shows, as well as telephone expenses (only those directly connected with judging activities such as calls to the AKC or show clubs), office supplies, books, subscriptions and miscellaneous expenses. All of these items are deductible by the professional judge and can be used against judging income for the hobby judge.

Ledgers are easily adapted to suit every circumstance and the maintainance of one solely for judging will help you in recording financial considerations connected with judging.

Receipts

Be sure to procure receipts for all expenses. This means not only motel/hotel bills, restaurant charges, air fares and auto rentals, but also toll and parking receipts, gas bills or mileage and so forth. The easiest way to keep track of all receipts is to charge everything. If you do a sufficient amount of judging, you should maintain a separate charge account for your expenses and only charge judging costs to that account. Don't use it for personal charges.

In checking out of a motel/hotel, instruct the clerk to staple the charge receipt to the bill. When eating in a restaurant with other judges, be sure to specify separate checks when your order is taken, saving later confusion. Keep all car rental slips with your charge receipt. Upon returning home for a show, make note of all expenses in your ledger and put all receipts in a file established for that purpose.

How you tabulate your automobile expenses depends on the age of the car, number of times used for judging and total costs. Automobile expenses can be taken strictly on a mileage basis, plus parking and tolls, with mileage computed from the time you leave your driveway to your return home. Or the car can be depreciated with actual gas, tires, oil, repairs, insurance and so forth pro-rated as to percentage of time used for shows and for personal use. Generally speaking you would only depreciate and pro-rate expenses if you judge frequently throughout the year. Whichever method you adopt, keep a small notebook in the glove compartment for jotting down mileage and other costs. By the way, mileage includes not only those shows where you drive directly to the event in your own vehicle, but also mileage used in getting to and from the airport, train station, etc.

Your 1040

Income tax time comes around all too quickly and how you claim your judging income and expenses depends entirely on your tax situation, the amount of judging during the year and the advice of your accountant or tax attorney.

The first point you will have to establish is whether you are a hobby judge or a business-professional judge. The general basis for establishing this point rests with your intention to be engaged in the enterprise for the purpose of making money and that you expect to do so for at least two out of seven consecutive years.

Judging as a Hobby

Most judges are hobby judges and therefore need merely to concern themselves with claiming the amount of money they received from shows, usually attributed to actual expenses, and then claiming those expenses as a deduction for a complete washout. It is important to remember that with a hobby, expenses can never exceed income derived from the hobby. The stopping figure for expenses is the income sum.

All income received from judging dog shows should be claimed under miscellaneous income with a brief notation—income received as dog show judge—and then the amount.

All expenses should be deducted under Schedule A, Miscellaneous Deductions. It may be necessary to use a separate sheet of plain white paper on which to show your expenses and compare them to the income figure previously reported, especially if your expenses exceed the income amount. You can only take that portion of the expenses that reach the income figure.

Professional Judge

Professional judges are those who charge a fee above all expenses and whose aim is to make a profit from their judging career. The money earned does not need to be the main source of income on which one lives, but is an amount in excess of expenses incurred.

In order to substantiate your status as a professional judge, you need to keep careful records of all judging income and expenses and maintain a separate checking account used solely for this purpose. All income received from shows should go into this account. You can pay draws to yourself as the money accumulates.

As a professional judge, you will be filing a Schedule C, self-employed business return with your regular 1040. This form is generally self-explanatory, with the exception that the amount for travel has to be broken down into separate categories. You can either take show by show, including transportation, meals and lodging, or lump the total yearly expenses under each separate heading. You may want to further define into sub-categories of airplane, train, auto rental and personal auto expenses. Once again, the car can be either deducted on mileage or pro-rated and depreciated on expenses and actual use. Tolls and parking charges should be included under another heading.

If you file as a professional judge, consult a tax man to assist you in setting up a system and filing a return. He will advise that there are many advantages to be derived from filing as a business, but you must exercise caution in being sure that you, a) qualify, b) maintain proper books and c) use those advantages to the utmost.

Taxes are never something to be taken lightly, so invest in the expertise needed to assist you in filing a proper return.

Department of the Treasury—Internal Revenue Service

U.S. Individual Income Tax Return 1979

ivacy Act Notice, see page 3 of Instructions | For the year January 1–December 31, 1979, or other tax year beginning , 1979, ending , 19

	Your first name and initial (if joint return, also give spouse's name and initial)	Last name	Your social security number

Present home address (Number and street, including apartment number, or rural route) | Spouse's social security no.

City, town or post office, State and ZIP code | Your occupation ▶ | Spouse's occupation ▶

dential on aign Fund

▶ Do you want $1 to go to this fund? . . . . | Yes | No | **Note:** Checking "Yes" will

If joint return, does your spouse want $1 to go to this fund? . . . | Yes | No | not increase your tax or reduce your refund.

g Status

only x.

1 ___ Single
2 ___ Married filing joint return (even if only one had income)
3 ___ Married filing separate return. Enter spouse's social security number above and full name here ▶ _____
4 ___ Head of household. (See page 7 of Instructions.) If qualifying person is your unmarried child, enter child's name ▶ _____
5 ___ Qualifying widow(er) with dependent child (Year spouse died ▶ 19). (See page 7 of Instructions.)

ptions

check x labeled lf. other if they

6a ___ Yourself ___ 65 or over ___ Blind } Enter number of boxes checked on 6a and b ▶ ___

b ___ Spouse ___ 65 or over ___ Blind

c First names of your dependent children who lived with you ▶ _____ } Enter number of children listed ▶ ___

d Other dependents: (1) Name	(2) Relationship	(3) Number of months lived in your home	(4) Did dependent have income of $1,000 or more?	(5) Did you provide more than one-half of dependent's support?	
					Enter number of other dependents ▶ ___
					Add numbers entered in boxes above ▶ ___

7 Total number of exemptions claimed . . . .

ne

attach B of your W–2 here.

do not have , see 5 of ctions.

8	Wages, salaries, tips, etc.	8	
9	Interest income *(attach Schedule B if over $400)*	9	
10a	Dividends *(attach Schedule B if over $400)*_____, 10b Exclusion_____		
c	Subtract line 10b from line 10a	10c	
11	State and local income tax refunds *(does not apply unless refund is for year you itemized deductions—see page 10 of Instructions)*.	11	
12	Alimony received	12	
13	Business income or (loss) *(attach Schedule C)*	13	
14	Capital gain or (loss) *(attach Schedule D)*	14	
15	Taxable part of capital gain distributions not reported on Schedule D (see page 10 of Instructions)	15	
16	Supplemental gains or (losses) *(attach Form 4797)*	16	
17	Fully taxable pensions and annuities not reported on Schedule E	17	
18	Pensions, annuities, rents, royalties, partnerships, estates or trusts, etc. *(attach Schedule E)*	18	
19	Farm income or (loss) *(attach Schedule F)*	19	
20a	Unemployment compensation. Total amount received_____		
b	Taxable part, if any, from worksheet on page 10 of Instructions	20b	
21	Other income *(state nature and source—see page 10 of Instructions)* ▶ _____ _____dog show judging fees_____	21	1615 00
22	**Total income.** Add amounts in column for lines 8 through 21 . . . . ▶	22	

stments come

se ch check oney r here.

23	Moving expense *(attach Form 3903 or 3903F)*	23		
24	Employee business expenses *(attach Form 2106)* . .	24		
25	Payments to an IRA *(see page 11 of Instructions)* . .	25		
26	Payments to a Keogh (H.R. 10) retirement plan . . .	26		
27	Interest penalty on early withdrawal of savings . . .	27		
28	Alimony paid *(see page 11 of Instructions)*	28		
29	Disability income exclusion *(attach Form 2440)* . . .	29		
30	**Total adjustments.** Add lines 23 through 29 . . . . ▶	30	

sted s Income

31 **Adjusted gross income.** Subtract line 30 from line 22. *If this line is less than $10,000, see page 2 of Instructions. If you want IRS to figure your tax, see page 4 of Instructions* . . . . ▶ | 31 |

Income entry for the hobby judge on his 1040

Schedules A&B—Itemized Deductions AND
Interest and Dividend Income

(Form 1040)
Department of the Treasury
Internal Revenue Service

▶ Attach to Form 1040.   ▶ See Instructions for Schedules A and B (Form 1040).

197.

08

Name(s) as shown on Form 1040 | Your social security num

Schedule A—Itemized Deductions *(Schedule B is on back)*

Medical and Dental Expenses (not paid or reimbursed by insurance or otherwise) *(See page 16 of Instructions.)*

1 One-half (but not more than $150) of insurance premiums you paid for medical care. (Be sure to include in line 10 below.) ▶

2 Medicine and drugs . . . . . .

3 Enter 1% of Form 1040, line 31 . . .

4 Subtract line 3 from line 2. If line 3 is more than line 2, enter zero . . . .

5 Balance of insurance premiums for medical care not entered on line 1 . . . .

6 Other medical and dental expenses:

a Doctors, dentists, nurses, etc. . . .

b Hospitals . . . .

c Other (itemize—include hearing aids, dentures, eyeglasses, transportation, etc.) ▶

7 Total (add lines 4 through 6c) . . . .

8 Enter 3% of Form 1040, line 31 . . .

9 Subtract line 8 from line 7. If line 8 is more than line 7, enter zero . . . .

10 Total medical and dental expenses (add lines 1 and 9). Enter here and on line 33 . ▶

Taxes *(See page 16 of Instructions.)*

Note: Gasoline taxes are no longer deductible.

11 State and local income . . . . . .

12 Real estate . . . .

13 General sales (see sales tax tables) . .

14 Personal property . . . .

15 Other (itemize) ▶

16 Total taxes (add lines 11 through 15). Enter here and on line 34 . . . . ▶

Interest Expense *(See page 17 of Instructions.)*

17 Home mortgage . . . .

18 Credit and charge cards . . . . .

19 Other (itemize) ▶

20 Total interest expense (add lines 17 through 19). Enter here and on line 35 ▶

Contributions *(See page 17 of Instructions.)*

21 a Cash contributions for which you have receipts, cancelled checks, or other written evidence . . . .

b Other cash contributions (show to whom you gave and how much you gave) ▶

22 Other than cash (see page 17 of instructions for required statement) . . . .

23 Carryover from prior years . . . . .

24 Total contributions (add lines 21a through 23). Enter here and on line 36 . ▶

Casualty or Theft Loss(es) *(See page 18 of Instructions.*

25 Loss before insurance reimbursement .

26 Insurance reimbursement . . . . .

27 Subtract line 26 from line 25. If line 26 is more than line 25, enter zero . . .

28 Enter $100 or amount from line 27, whichever is smaller . . . . . .

29 Total casualty or theft loss(es) (subtract line 28 from line 27). Enter here and on line 37 . ▶

Miscellaneous Deductions *(See page 18 of Instructions.)*

30 Union dues . . . .

31 Other (itemize) ▶
dog show judges expenses
(see attached explanation)   1615

32 Total miscellaneous deductions (add lines 30 and 31). Enter here and on line 38 ▶

Summary of Itemized Deductions
(See page 18 of Instructions.)

33 Total medical and dental—from line 10 .

34 Total taxes—from line 16 . . . . .

35 Total interest—from line 20 . . . .

36 Total contributions—from line 24 . . .

37 Total casualty or theft loss(es)—from line 29 .

38 Total miscellaneous—from line 32 . . .

39 Add lines 33 through 38 . . . . .

40 If you checked Form 1040, Filing Status box:
2 or 5, enter $3,400 . . . .
1 or 4, enter $2,300 . . . .
3, enter $1,700 . . . . .

41 Subtract line 40 from line 39. Enter here and on Form 1040, line 33. (If line 40 is more than line 39, see the instructions for line 41 on page 18.) . . . . . ▶

Expense deduction for the hobby judge on Schedule A, Form 1040

John Q. Judge   1978
Smithtown Road   SS# 330-00-0000
Pottersville, OH 27840

Form 1040, Schedule A

Miscellaneous Deductions:

31. Other -

Taxpayer, John Q. Judge, incurred travel expenses
in connection with his hobby as a dog show judge. Income
from same is listed herein as other income, line 20, 1040
in the amount of $1,615.00, for the five shows he judged
during 1978. Total travel expenses from taxpayer's
residence to San Mesa, Ca., Hyde Park, NY, Jason City, Fl.,
Stewardsville, Oh. and Brownstown, Ill. is:

Air fares	-	1,017.00
Mileage 1257 mi.	-	214.00
Tolls, parking and limo	-	64.00
Motels/Hotels	-	227.00
Meals	-	93.00

Total Hobby expenses -------------$ 1,615.00

**Sample supplemental sheet to attach to Schedule A
explaining the miscellaneous deduction for your hobby**

SCHEDULE C (Form 1040)

Department of the Treasury
Internal Revenue Service

Profit or (Loss) From Business or Profession

(Sole Proprietorship)

Partnerships, Joint Ventures, etc., Must File Form 1065.

▶ Attach to Form 1040 or Form 1041.   ▶ See Instructions for Schedule C (Form 1040).

1979

09

Name of proprietor: John Q. Judge

Social security number of proprietor: 000 00 0000

A Main business activity (see Instructions) ▶ dog show judge   ; product ▶

B Business name ▶

C Employer identification number: none

D Business address (number and street) ▶
City, State and Zip Code ▶

E Accounting method: (1) ☒ Cash   (2) ☐ Accrual   (3) ☐ Other (specify) ▶

F Method(s) used to value closing inventory:

   (1) ☐ Cost   (2) ☐ Lower of cost or market   (3) ☐ Other (if other, attach explanation)

	Yes	
G Was there any major change in determining quantities, costs, or valuations between opening and closing inventory? If "Yes," attach explanation.		
H Did you deduct expenses for an office in your home?		
I Did you elect to claim amortization (under section 191) or depreciation (under section 167(o)) for a rehabilitated certified historic structure (see Instructions)? (Amortizable basis (see Instructions) ▶)		

Part I   Income

1 a Gross receipts or sales	**1a**	18456 00	
b Returns and allowances	**1b**		
c Balance (subtract line 1b from line 1a)		**1c**	18456
2 Cost of goods sold and/or operations (Schedule C–1, line 8)		**2**	
3 Gross profit (subtract line 2 from line 1c)		**3**	18456
4 Other income (attach schedule)		**4**	
5 Total income (add lines 3 and 4) ▶		**5**	18456

Part II   Deductions

6 Advertising		**31 a** Wages		
7 Amortization		**b** Jobs credit		
8 Bad debts from sales or services		**c** WIN credit		
9 Bank charges	9 00	**d** Total credits		
10 Car and truck expenses 59.74 mi	1105 00	**e** Subtract line 31d from 31a		
11 Commissions		**32** Other expenses (specify):		
12 Depletion		**a** As a judge of pure-bred dogs,		
13 Depreciation (explain in Schedule C–2)		**b** taxpayer traveled throughout		
14 Dues and publications	168 00	**c** the US & Canada to 40 shows		
15 Employee benefit programs		**d** during 1979:		
16 Freight (not included on Schedule C–1)		**e** air fares	4135 0	
17 Insurance		**f** parking, tolls	234 0	
18 Interest on business indebtedness		**g** auto rental & limo	1694 0	
19 Laundry and cleaning	120 00	**h** motel/hotel	1687 0	
20 Legal and professional services	150 00	**i** meals away from home	748 0	
21 Office supplies	337 00	**j**		
22 Pension and profit-sharing plans		**k**		
23 Postage	68 00	**l**		
24 Rent on business property		**m**		
25 Repairs	83 00	**n**		
26 Supplies (not included on Schedule C–1)		**o**		
27 Taxes		**p**		
28 Telephone	683 00	**q**		
29 Travel and entertainment		**r**		
30 Utilities		**s**		

33 Total deductions (add amounts in columns for lines 6 through 32s) ▶	**33**	11221 0	
34 Net profit or (loss) (subtract line 33 from line 5). If a profit, enter on Form 1040, line 13, and on Schedule SE, Part II, line 5a (or Form 1041, line 6). If a loss, go on to line 35	**34**	7235 0	
35 If you have a loss, do you have amounts for which you are **not** "at risk" in this business (see Instructions)? ☐ Yes ☐			

Business return Schedule C, Form 1040, for the professional judge

17

Junior Showmanship

JUDGING JUNIOR SHOWMANSHIP is diametrically opposite to judging confirmation classes. Instead of ignoring the handler and judging the quality of the dog, in JS you judge the expertise of the handler and ignore the animal's merit or lack thereof.

It used to be that you could judge the kids by what they did not do, such as moving out of the way so as not to block the judge's view of their dogs, or keeping the animal's feet correctly positioned. Judging JS was then an elimination contest—whoever showed their dog as you thought it should be shown came up a winner. In recent years, however, the kids have become so good that it is nearly impossible to find fault with their showmanship methods. This makes it extremely difficult to narrow down choices to just four children for each class, realizing that a majority of the entrants demonstrate superb showmanship techniques.

Due to the above, JS is best judged on one of two bases:

a) give your highest awards to the kids that you notice the least on the theory that handlers should not be seen although their presence is felt, or

b) mentally evaluate each dog's faults and observe what its junior handler does to hide that fault from you and whether he succeeds or fails.

199

APPLICATION TO JUDGE JUNIOR SHOWMANSHIP

This application is to be completed by persons 17 years of age or over who would like approval to judge Junior Showmanship at AKC licensed or member shows.

Name (Print) _____ Date of Birth _____

Complete Home Address _____

_____ Home Phone _____

Occupation _____ Business Phone _____

I. 1. Do you handle dogs professionally according to the following definition?:
Professional Handlers — all persons who represent themselves through a rate card or otherwise as handling dogs in the show ring for pay. _____ Yes _____ No

2. Do you reside in the same household with a Professional Handler? _____

If so, state Handler's name _____

3. Do you or any member of your immediate family or household prepare, condition or handle dogs for others? _____

Are you (they) compensated in any way? _____ If yes to either or both, please explain. _____

_____

_____

4. Do you presently own or operate a pet shop or grooming business. _____ If yes, give location and number of years in business. _____

5. Do you or any member of your immediate household maintain a boarding kennel? _____ If yes, indicate location how long you (they) have been operating it and if dogs boarded are show specimens or pets.

_____

_____

6. Are you now or have you ever been employed in and about kennels? _____ If yes, please give details (including dates) _____

_____

_____

7. Do you buy dogs for resale? _____ If yes, please explain in detail.

_____

_____

Do you buy dogs to improve your breeding stock? _____ In instances where you sell dogs, do you furnish the buyers with American Kennel Club applications for registration? _____ If no, please explain. _____

_____

_____

_____

8. Are you connected in any way with a publication disseminating dog news or carrying dog advertising? _____

If yes, please give complete details. _____

_____

_____

_____

**Junior Showmanship Application for persons over
17 who wish to apply to judge Juniors only.**

9. Are you connected in any way with a dog food, dog remedy or kennel supply company?_____ If yes, give complete details._____

_____

_____

_____

10. Have you ever been suspended from the privileges of The American Kennel Club?_____If so, state the date and circumstances. _____

_____

_____

_____

II. Information to be completed by former Junior Showmanship competitors:

1. When did you first compete in Junior Showmanship at licensed or member shows?

_____

2. When did you first compete in the Open Class in Junior Showmanship?

_____

3. Approximately how many times did you compete in the Open Class?

_____

4. What breeds did you handle in Junior Showmanship? _____

_____

5. List licensed or member shows (by club name and date) at which you won awards in Junior Showmanship during your last two years as a Junior Showmanship competitor.

_____

_____

_____

_____

****

III. Information to be completed by all Junior Showmanship Judging Applicants:

1. Have you judged Junior Showmanship competition at any AKC Sanctioned matches? _____If so, identify the events by club name and date, giving the entry in each instance.

_____

_____

_____

2. If you have worked in an official capacity at any AKC licensed or member shows or any AKC sanctioned matches, identify the events and state capacity in which you served.

_____

_____

_____

_____

3. Describe any other activities in the sport of dogs. _____

_____

_____

_____

4. Give names and addresses of 2 persons who could attest to your knowledge of ring procedure and handling procedures. _____

_____

_____

5. Describe in detail what your procedure would be in judging a class of 15 Junior Handlers from the time they enter
the ring until they leave the ring.

_____

_____

_____

_____

_____

_____

6. What are the qualities that you would look for in judging Junior Showmanship?

_____

_____

_____

_____

7. Explain in your own words why you feel you are qualified to judge Junior Showmanship.

_____

_____

_____

I hereby submit this application to the Board of Directors of the American Kennel Club for their consideration and make the following representations:

That I am not occupationally ineligible to judge under the provisions of Chapter 10, Section 1 (Dog Show Rules) which reads: "Any reputable person who is in good standing with The American Kennel Club may apply for leave to judge any breed or breeds of pure-bred dogs which in his or her opinion he or she is qualified by training and experience to pass upon, with the exception of persons connected with any publication in the capacity of solicitor for kennel advertisements, persons connected with dog food, dog remedy or kennel supply companies in the capacity of solicitor or salesman, persons employed in and about kennels, persons who buy, sell and in any way trade or traffic in dogs as a means of livelihood in whole or in part, whether or not they be known as dealers."

That I will at all times judge in accord with the current official standards and in strict conformity with the applicable dog show rules, regulations and ring procedures as are in force at the time of the dog show that I am judging.

Marital Status_____ Name of Spouse _____

Date _____ Signature of Applicant _____

The latter is perhaps the better method as long as you possess the background and knowledge. JS is a contest of handlers, albeit young amateurs, whose purpose is to present dogs at their best; to mold, bend and show them so that what a judge observes are animals at the top of their form in showmanship and condition.

There are some judges who agree to take JS assignments although they have had no experience either with kids or the theory behind the formulation of this classification. This is unfortunate as everyone is cheated in the end. It behooves all persons who are desirous of judging JS to fully acquaint themselves with all aspects of this task. Write to the AKC for a copy of the booklet entitled *Regulations for Junior Showmanship*.

JS is no longer automatically granted. Conformation judges approved for one or more breeds check a box on their original approval letter advising the AKC if they want to judge JS. Juniors, themselves, may apply to judge JS only after they have reached their seventeenth birthday by writing to the AKC, requesting an Application to Judge Junior Showmanship.

Many judges may prefer not to adjudicate juniors for one or all of the following reasons:

a) lack of knowhow
b) unable to be objective in choosing between children
c) unwilling to subject themselves to verbal confrontations by over-zealous parents of losing kids.

One must applaud this decision to be honest with oneself, and it is only when all parties involved step back and apply tangible reasons, such as these, that the stigma attached to JS will fade away. Don't apply to judge JS merely to offer additional entries to prospective clubs. Rather apply because you are genuinely interested in furthering the advancement of junior handlers. You must be willing to judge objectively with forethought and knowledge and truly feel comfortable dealing with children.

18

AKC Viewpoint

Individual interviews with various officers of the American Kennel Club offer evidence of their serious interest in the present and future of dog show judges in America. Aware of problems confronting the new judge, undercurrents that exist in the sport and sometimes seemingly contradictory policies, the AKC is endeavoring to make changes as necessary, clarifications where needed and to recognize the strengths and weaknesses that exist within the system.

The following are blended excerpts of separate interviews covering the areas of education and standards, approval procedures and overall goals for judges with persons directly responsible for the status of judging today: William F. Stifel, President; Charles A. T. O'Neill, Executive Vice-President; and William M. Schmick, Vice-President in charge of show operations:

"Education is a must and national breed clubs can play a vital role in helping our judges by sponsoring judging seminars in which their breed would be discussed in depth and from various points by breeders, exhibitors, handlers and other judges. Just as important is an understanding of the standards by judges and breeders alike. Some are rather general while others describe certain aspects almost to the point of exhaustion and omit other parts of the dog almost entirely. Some are models and are held up as such.

"Breed clubs are the keepers of their standards and we must

studiously avoid legislating changes other than restraints and guidelines. However, standards, like most documents, can be revised and would benefit from an on-going study by a standard's committee comprised of really knowledgeable breeders making recommendations, not to accommodate dogs that are winning in the ring, but to fill in some missing gaps and clarify comments or preferences on markings, colors, gait or anything else where the written words are not absolutely clear. On the other hand, clubs must refrain from becoming too detailed or putting too much in a standard leaving one suspicious that they are describing not an ideal specimen but something in their own kennel. A breed standard should serve as a general outline of a reminder. It is not meant, first of all, for people who don't know anything about the breed; rather it is meant for people who, in fact, know quite a bit about it. It should serve as an outline of the various factors in that breed which make it unique, point out certain dangerous areas to be aware of and extreme faults which may be a real problem in the breed that judges must be particularly careful to eliminate. The standard, therefore, must be a guideline to remind judges of particular aspects of the breed.

"Conflicts are other problems facing judges. Both the two-hundred-mile, thirty-day restriction and disagreements with clubs as to what was actually agreed upon are areas that can be easily managed.

"The two-hundred-mile, thirty-day restriction is simple enough to keep track of if you have a controlled, up-to-date calendar that you readily consult. If in doubt as to the distance between two assignments, don't hesitate to call the show plans department at the AKC.

"Problems experienced with clubs result primarily because conversations with show chairmen are not confirmed in writing. A date should be reserved on the strength of a phone call, subject to written confirmation within a reasonable period of time, such as ten days or two weeks. Judges should then respond to that written invitation promptly, spelling out in their response what they expect in terms of expenses and/or fee and what they also expect from the clubs in form of services such as whether or not they need to be met at an airport or railroad station and then transported the remaining fifteen or twenty miles to the show site or motel. This avoids many of the unpleasantries that arise the day before a show, or morning of a show, when people are stranded at airports or train stations wondering where their transportation is coming from. It would help a great deal if all arrangements are firmed up in writing, which should remove any hassling on the day of the show about costs/fee, and what was agreed upon or thought was going to be done by both the judges and the show-giving club.

"Judges also have to learn how to deal with complaining exhibitors. Sometimes they are afraid to be frank and this weakness is exploited by the exhibitor. Experienced judges are not such an easy target since they become quite adept in handling situations as they arise. It is also true that the more one judges, the easier the task becomes. He no longer has to think about judging procedure and is inherently aware of soundness and breed standards.

"New judges do have difficulties getting started. In the beginning stages, they receive either local invitations or pay their own expenses to distant shows because clubs cannot afford to, or don't want to pay for judges doing only one or two breeds. It is also understood that chairmen are reluctant to pick unknown persons out of the book. Presumably judges are suggested by club members who knew the person as a breeder or through personal contacts. It is known, however, that there is such a thing as swapping assignments. AKC frowns on this and has spoken out against it numerous times.

"It is certainly not within the contemplation of the Kennel Club at this time to stop approving judges as we did with the delicensing of handlers. This is a large country with many, many events and we need a governing body to approve and regulate our judges. For example, a show chairman might be able to pick out ideal persons in his immediate neighborhood who could judge a handful of breeds, but to ask him to pick out persons for 124 would be unrealistic. Someone has got to do some of that work for him and what we are really trying to do is to give guidance.

"Our procedure of approving judges may not be perfect, but it is better than anything anyone has been able to come up with. We aim to get as much input as we can on possible judges, both from the fancy and our own people via the use of personal interviews and observations.

"In the case of both provisional judging applicants and applicants for additional breeds AKC is now conducting a personal interview. This interview is designed to give the judging applicant an opportunity to ask questions of the AKC on a one-to-one basis and to thoroughly understand the procedure for approval including what qualifications are desired. It has been found that such a discussion is considerably more enlightening for both the AKC and the judging applicant than the old written application. A common misapprehension, however, is that this interview is the most important factor in AKC's decision. As a matter of fact, it is only one part and in the case of applicants for additional breeds the reports of field representatives on the judge's actual performance in the ring continue to be the most critical factor. Similarly, in the case of provisional applicants, basic breeding, exhibiting, stewarding and match show judging are clearly the most important factors in a final decision. On the other hand, in the interviewing situation it has been found that considerable information can be obtained on exactly how well the applicant has prepared himself for the task of judging the breeds involved. Not the least important thing that is able to be determined is whether or not judges have formed a very specific picture in their minds of the ideal specimen of any given breed. This is often best determined by getting the applicant to give his opinion of great dogs of the past or recent history. It is felt that the holding of strong opinions is crucial to being consistent in judging and judges who are consistent in the type that they select clearly incur the least criticism. Different judges interpret breed standards differently and that is the whole basis of the sport of dogs. That is why one dog wins on one day and another on the next with identical competition. It has been found in the interviews that the degree of a judge's breed knowledge and specific preference for the kind of dog he is looking for in a given breed can be determined without questioning the applicant in terms of right or wrong answers.

"Many of the applicants for additional breeds interviewed in the first year of its use approached it with doubt if not hostility. Yet having completed just over a year of doing these interviews it can be stated unqualified that the technique is successful.

"In observing judges, the field representatives are primarily looking for proper ring procedure and control, knowledge of the rules and consistency in selections. The reps should be able to follow the judge given enough, and this is the real catch, enough dogs of a similar type from which to select. They do not have to agree with the decision, but have to have confidence that the judge is accomplishing a workmanlike job by doing the very best with what he has in the ring at that time.

"Just as the functions of the field reps' interviews and observations are often misunderstood, so too are the various rules and policies directed towards judicial behavior. Most of these are aimed at protecting the judge, who at times can be his own worst enemy. We try to keep them out of situations and circumstances that can be extremely unpleasant for them, which is why we don't like them to attend judges' dinners the night before a show when exhibitors are going to be present, or be overly friendly with exhibitors or handlers the day of the show, to name but a few circumstances that could lead some observer to assume that that particular judge's decision is based on reasonings other than objective ones. We encourage the use of good common sense and good taste in dealing with situations that might arise.

"In the ring, our judges should conduct themselves as ladies and gentlemen; present an appearance that is neat and comfortable for a sporting occasion; run their rings with decorum; be firm in their decisions, yet pleasant; and leave no doubt in anyone's mind as to what they are there for—to pick what they genuinely feel are the best specimens that have been produced and brought before them to be judged on that day."

As you can see, the purpose of the interviews was not to zero in on what the AKC is or is not doing for the sport, but rather to seek an explanation of some of the reasons why things are done as they are and what is expected of our judges in and out of the ring.

19

What Happens If

. . . you don't want to accept any assignment to judge at a particular show?

A——You are under no obligation to accept each and every assignment that comes your way. It is not uncommon for judges to turn down invitations from clubs that have a reputation of not taking care of their judges or putting too many restrictions on them.

. . . you receive a phone call and/or letter from a show chairman asking if you would be available to judge his show on such and such a date without any definite breed assignment?

A——If you are not free on that day, tell him so. Or, if you have a conflict with certain breeds, advise him of this. If you are totally free, accept the assignment giving your fee and/or expense and request a reply from him within a specified length of time (two to four weeks) confirming the assignment with definite breeds, Groups or Best In Show.

. . . a judge receives another invitation but has enough breeds to split between the two clubs that would otherwise be in conflict?

A——He should then telephone the chairmen to procure definite assignment commitments from both clubs regarding which breeds, groups and/or BIS he is to officiate at each show.

208

. . . you do not hear anything further from that club?

A——Feel free to accept other assignments as long as the waiting period has passed. If and when you do receive a positive commitment and you are still open, accept the show. If not, write back and tell the club that you are no longer available.

. . . a club asked you to judge at their show sometime ago, either on the phone or in person, and you accepted the assignment subject to written confirmation within a specified period of time. Not having heard anything further, you went ahead and accepted another show. Now all of a sudden you find out from the chairman of the second show that the AKC says you have a conflict with the first show which had not been confirmed. What do you do?

A——Tell the show chairman of the second show to sit tight for a few days while you try to straighten the situation out. Call Show Plans at the AKC, advise them of what transpired between you and both clubs: that you did not have a confirmed acceptance from the first club, but do have one from the second show. If at all possible, they will release you from the first show leaving you free to judge the second show as planned. Call that chairman back and advise him of the same.

. . . you had no conflict with a second show and the first thing you knew about judging the first show was when you received a copy of the premium list in the mail. What is your option?

A——Although you don't have to do so, it would be helpful if you could see you way through to do the show, even though you may be madder than heck at the club. However, if you have personal obligations that prevent you from being available, contact Show Plans and take it from there.

. . . the show chairman never receives a response from the judge he contacted?

A——If the letter was for a definite assignment, as opposed to a letter of inquiry regarding fees charged, the chairman should receive an immediate reply. If he does not hear from the prospective judge within a reasonable period of time, he may follow up his letter with a phone call in case the correspondence never reached the judge. He also has the option of choosing another judge.

. . . a show in Michigan is 230 driving miles from one in Wisconsin, can you judge the same assignment at both shows?

A——No, driving miles do not count. The restriction is placed on two hundred straight-line miles, thirty days, even though a large body of water that cannot be crossed by auto is in the way. Call Show Plans if you have any questions about distances.

. . . the AKC says that two shows are less than two hundred miles from each other even though both your and the club's calculations come to over two hundred miles?
A——There is nothing you can do. AKC word is final in this, even if variances exist.

. . . you are already committed to officiate at a show for a specified sum representing fee and/or expenses and you move across the country?
A——Contact the show chairmen of those clubs where your expenses are going to be a great deal higher than anticipated prior to the move and advise him of the same. If the club is not willing to absorb the additional amount, you have no choice but to make up the difference out of your own pocket.

. . . you wish to include as your expenses figure not only transportation, lodging and meals, but also the cost of someone to take care of your dogs while away from home, or other personal expenses. Can you?
A——Yes, as long as you advise the show-giving club of exactly what constitutes expenses, or give them an estimated sum over and above transportation, lodging and meals that will cover your peripheral expenses.

. . . someone else's entry drew an overload and you are asked to take on additional breeds?
A——The key word here is *asked*. Clubs should advise their judges in advance of any changes, additions or subtractions that directly affect them and get their OK.

. . . you drew a small entry. Do you still have to judge?
A——Yes, you have a confirmed obligation to judge at that show regardless of the size of your entry. Swallow your pride and judge to the best of your ability.

. . . someone forgot to pick you up at the airport or motel?

210

A——Although previous arrangements may have been made, it is still the judge's responsibility to get wherever he has to be. Call the hospitality chairman to see what the problem is or rent a car, hire a cab, assessing the expense to the club, as you do whatever is necessary to get you to the motel or show grounds.

. . . you become sick the morning of the show and are unable to judge?
A——Contact the show chairman, member of the judge's committee, hospitality member or anyone else from the club. If you cannot raise a member, leave messages and ask to have word immediately passed on to the show grounds. If you are staying at the same motel as the superintendent, AKC field rep, or other judges, try to get word to them. Let someone know that you are ill and will not be able to make it.

. . . you fouled up and had the wrong date, wrong city or wrong show and totally missed the show you were contracted for?
A——Your only recourse is to apologize to the club and offer to judge its show the following year free of charge. You can also contact the AKC to explain your error. This way they know you did not miss the show intentionally and as long as it is your first and last time, you shouldn't be heavily penalized.

. . . at the end of the show you forget to pick up your check?
A——Most clubs will mail your check to you, but call the show chairman as soon as you return home asking to have it sent. To avoid this necessity make every effort to see the club treasurer before you leave the grounds. Search him out if need be as this very often becomes the judge's burden.

. . . the club does not want to pay you the sum agreed upon or reimburse expenses.
A——Show the treasurer the correspondence you have had with the club, which you carry with you. In your final contractual agreement with the club the financial conditions should be clearly stated.

. . . the club's check bounces?
A——Merely redeposit the check. Chances are there was a crossing of funds and the check should clear the second time around. If it doesn't, contact the club and the AKC for assistance.

. . . it is time for you to start judging and you have no steward to assist you?

A——If at five minutes prior to starting time, you do not see a steward in your ring, let the show chairman or other responsible club person know you have a potential problem. When starting time comes and help has not arrived, be prepared to handle the matter by yourself. If the steward's bag containing armbands, ribbons and awards is not on the table, have the superintendent/show secretary bring it over immediately. If it is there, or once it arrives, delve into the bag yourself, bringing everything out but the catalog. Hand out the armbands for the first class using the numbers appearing in your judge's book. Sort your ribbons and awards and proceed to judge. Chances are someone will eventually show up to give you a hand. If not, make the best of it.

. . . a dog is entered in the wrong class?

A——A dog entered in the wrong class can be changed at the show only if a) the error was due to sex, or b) the error was made by the superintendent/show secretary. Call that official to ringside and have him make the necessary correction in your book.

. . . a wrong number is allocated to a particular dog in your book?

A——This error is noticed when a dog comes into the ring with an armband number that does not appear in your book for that particular class. There will be a rechecking of the number with the steward and his catalog by the exhibitor. If it appears that accordingly the number is correct, the superintendent/show secretary must come to the ring to correct the error that appears in your judge's book. Errors of this type are administrative and not judicial which is why the corrections are not made by the judge.

. . . a dog is known to be present on the grounds but not yet in the ring when the class is called. Should you wait for the missing dog?

A——No, you should not wait for anyone. Commence judging and if the dog arrives before you have finished individually examining and individually gaiting all the animals in the ring, you may wish to let the latecomer in. It is important to note that is is the judge's option to let a latecomer into the ring any time prior to marking his book. You do not have to let him in the ring at all and this is true even if you have just started the class. Similarly, you can let him in when you are having the dogs go through a final gait around the ring. This, however, opens the judge up to criticism, especially if he awards a ribbon to the latecomer who is extremely late in coming.

. . . the steward tells you the missing dog is on the grounds but not in the ring because the owner had to go over to the superintendent's office to straighten out a bad check which he gave for the entry. Do you wait for this dog?

A——No. Begin to judge the class even though you know the dog is present on the grounds. Follow the same procedure listed above. Your steward should not have said anything about why the animal was not there, even though he knew of the matter because the superintendent placed a note instead of the corresponding armband to get the offender to come to the office and cover the funds.

. . . the only dog entered in a breed arrives during his hour's segment but after his scheduled slot and you have already marked the dog absent in your book?

A——As long as the dog is owned by one person and is at the ringside before the end of his scheduled hour, you have the option to go ahead and judge the dog even though you have already marked him absent in your book. When advised by the steward that the absent breed dog is at ringside during his hour, you can either agree to judge him or not. If you do not want to, fine. Your book will stand as already written. If, however, you acquiesce, advise the steward that you will judge the dog, preferably at the end of the hour before starting the next segment. When you judge the dog, mark and initial all changes in your judge's book reflecting the award(s) given and time alterations.

. . . the dog that placed second to the Winners Dog in its class does not return for reserve winners judging.

A——You shouldn't wait any longer than a minute or two for this missing dog. If it does not appear, judge reserve without him. Mark your book accordingly.

. . . the Winners Dog or Bitch does not return to the ring for Best of Breed/Variety judging and subsequent Best of Winners determination?

A——There is no Best of Winners.

. . . the missing Winners shows up after you finished BOB/BOS judging, can you then judge BOW?

A——Once you have marked your book showing completion of that judging segment, you cannot later judge BOW. Only if the missing Winners shows up prior to your having marked the book can you permit the dog in the ring for BOW judging.

. . . a dog is entered in two regular classes and marked absent for the first one. Is he still eligible to compete in the second class?
A——AKC policy is that you should let him be shown under the theory that denial of that right to be judged cannot be compensated at a later date. It will be up to show records to decide if any award given should be disallowed or not.

. . . a dog is entered in both open class and BOB competition, must he compete in both?
A——He must compete in open class initially and cannot be denied the right to BOB competition regardless of the placement in open. If the animal wins the latter and loses the former, it will be up to show records to determine if the win stands or not.

. . . in a specialty show, a dog is absent for a non-regular class but shows up in time for the regular classes?
A——This dog can still be shown in the regular classes. For example, even if he missed sweepstakes, he can still be shown in puppy class.

. . . at a specialty show where there is a Best Puppy in Show award, does the puppy who wins Winners Dog/Bitch in regular class automatically become Best Puppy?
A——If the judging of all non-regular and regular classes takes place on the same day under the same judge, yes. If the specialty is spread over two or more days and/or with different judges for dog and bitch classes, then the answer is no, and Best Puppy will have to be judged as a separate class irrespective of higher wins.

. . . you really don't want to permit handlers into your ring to take over their dogs once you have started judging a class and have not finished individually examining and individually gaiting every dog?
A——That's OK. The decision rests with the judge on whether handler takeovers are permitted and no reason for denial has to be given.

. . . the show committee wants to move your ring during breed judging?

214

A——Generally rings may be moved during a good breaking point such as between sexes or prior to BOB/V competition. However in a crisis situation, rings can be moved at any time.

. . . You withhold a ribbon or ribbons?
A——When a ribbon is withheld for any reason with no ribbon at all being awarded rather than a 2nd, 3rd or 4th in a one dog class, then that dog does not count for championship points. Similarly if in a large class, a judge chooses to award a 1st, 2nd and 3rd, but withholds 4th, then all of the dogs that did not receive a ribbon do not count toward points.

. . . you excuse or disqualify a dog?
A——The dog does not count toward points.

. . . you suspect a dog is blind in one eye?
A——You may penalize him accordingly, but he can only be disqualified if neither eye has useful sight.

. . . you're not sure whether a dog can hear?
A——Test for hearing by quietly making a sound or whistling. If he hears you, he will respond by cocking his head, brightening his eyes or even backing off if the noise frightens him.

. . . you have trouble checking an animal's teeth?
A——Have the exhibitor show you the teeth to your satisfaction. If this cannot be done, excuse the dog and mark your book accordingly.

. . . an exhibitor asks you if he can show you the bite, or you prefer him to do so?
A——Showing of the bite, like teeth, is the judge's prerogative. Usually you wouldn't mind if an exhibitor shows you the bite so long as you get to see the bite and not a clever trick of handling that disguises a faulty mouth. Be on guard for this, as well as the common story that "My dog has a sore throat today." Be sure you can see the bite to your satisfaction and if not, excuse the animal.

. . . you want to re-examine three toy dogs on the table at once for comparison purposes?
A——You can't do this even though you may have already had them individually on the table. Place two on the table at a time, if you wish,

and then remove the one that is no longer in contention, placing the third in his spot.

. . . you wish to stop examining the dogs on the table half-way through a breed?
A——This is not permissible. Once you started judging dogs of a given breed on the table, all others must also be examined on the table. Conversely, if you started examining dogs on the ground, you cannot decide to use the table in the middle of a breed.

. . . you want to know how old a dog is?
A——Ask your steward to give you the birth date out of the catalog for dog # so and so. Then you compute the age from the birthdate.

. . . you want to go back and recheck bite, shoulders, hindquarters or what have you on one or two dogs, do you have to recheck all the dogs?
A——No. Only check those dogs that you question. Once you have initially examined and gaited all of the dogs in a class, the equal treatment standard has been met. Anything else is extra and applies only to those animals actually under contention. You need not play to either the exhibitor, owner or audience.

. . . there is a puppy or novice dog that is either really scared or regards the ring as a romping area. Do you have to gait him exactly as you did the other dogs in the class?
A——No. First try to use your normal pattern. If that doesn't work, be flexible and patient as you try another area of the ring and different pattern.

. . . the best dog in the class is totally misbehaving?
A——If you can, get your hands on him checking him over as thoroughly as you did the other dogs in the class. Take extra time to reassure the animal. Have him regait until you see that he can put four feet on the ground. If you can't get your hands on him, or he will not gait well enough for you to be sure he is not lame, you have no choice but to excuse the dog.

. . . you tell an exhibitor to place his dog in a particular spot and the instructions are either ignored or the dog is moved when your back is turned?

216

A——Go back, be firm and issue your instructions again. If you still have a lack of cooperation, excuse the dog.

. . . you are grouping dogs and an exhibitor jumps ahead of line during the go round or when your back is turned?
A——If you are down to your final decision, skip him entirely and place the dogs as you would have if he had stayed where he belonged. Don't be intimidated by an overly aggressive person who is trying to pull a fast one on you.

. . . you have told an exhibitor to gait his dog on a loose lead or more slowly and he ignores your request?
A——Tell him again and if he continues to ignore you, excuse the dog. Always remember that you are the boss of your ring and as such should tolerate only so much. You have the option to excuse anyone who refuses to obey your instructions as long as your requests are reasonable.

. . . you have already made an initial cut in a class and want to make another. Can you do this?
A——Yes, you can make as many cuts as you deem necessary but never leave yourself with less than five or six dogs for the four placements.

. . . a dog comes into the ring with bandages on his body?
A——This dog should be excused as you really don't know what is under the bandages.

. . . if a dog is excused for being lame in sweepstakes, can it still be shown in regular classes?
A——If the sweepstakes and regular classes are held on the same day, no. A dog excused for being lame is excused for the day. If the regular classes are held on the next day, however, he is eligible to compete.

. . . a dog tries to bite you?
A——Excuse him.

. . . tries to bite his handler?
A——Excuse him.

. . . tries to bite another dog?

A——Excuse him. You cannot condone viciousness, nor place your-self, other exhibitors and dogs in jeopardy. Even sparring terriers should be carefully watched and the dogs kept under control. If the breed standard is such that viciousness is a disqualification, then you should disqualify instead of excusing the animal.

. . . an exhibitor tries to draw you into a debate regarding your decision to excuse or disqualify his dog?

A——Don't let it happen. Be firm and send the offender out of your ring. If he continues to argue with you, call for a show committee hearing.

. . . the judge who has your assigned ring before you falls far behind schedule?

A——There is nothing you can do other than look around to see if there is an empty ring. If so, suggest to the show chairman, not the field rep, that he consider letting you use the free ring.

. . . a group you are judging is called even though one of the breeds is not finished being judged?

A——Go ahead and start. Ten minutes is usually the time frame allowed for a breed to finish and a group to begin. By the time the other dogs are checked in and all paperwork done, the breed should be over. If not, it will be shortly.

. . . a dog goes lame in group or best in show competition?

A——Excuse him.

. . . is vicious in group or BIS?

A——Excuse him.

. . . is found to be missing a testicle, or have some other general or breed disqualification, in group or BIS?

A——He should be disqualified.

. . . you find an excessive amount of chalk, hairspray or cleaning substance on an animal?

A——Excuse the dog.

. . . you question the color of a dog for the class division he is entered in?

218

A——If you believe the dog is of the wrong color for that particular class, he must be excused. He will not be eligible for another class on that day.

   . . . the color is such that is it a disqualifying factor in the breed standard.
A——Disqualify the dog under Chapter 18, Section 6.

   . . . the Winners dog or bitch goes lame in BOB/V competition?
A——The animal must be excused from further competition and there will be no BOW award.

   . . . a dog is excused in group or BIS competition?
A——He keeps all awards and points, if any, won up to that time.

   . . . a dog is disqualified in group or BIS competition?
A——He loses all previous awards and points, if any, won at that time.

   . . . you want to buy your own wicket to carry and use in your ring?
A——You may purchase a wicket or set of wickets for your own use from the AKC. But you may not use any other wicket than the model officially prescribed for measuring.

   . . . you wish to use your hands as a means of measuring dogs to see if you need to call for the wicket. Is this permissible?
A——Yes, use your hands, mark your pantsleg or skirt to assist you in making a preliminary determination. But you can only disqualify on size after you have actually measured the dog with the proper wicket.

   . . . a dog won't stand still for measuring after a reasonable period of trying?
A——Excuse the animal, marking your book "Excused - unable to measure."

   . . . you desire to measure a dog of a breed where the standard specifies that any dog over a certain height should be severely penalized?
A——You cannot use the wicket on any breeds other than those where height disqualifications exist in their standards. In all other

breeds you have to rely on your eyes to guide you in proper size measurements.

. . . someone tries to challenge your measurement?
A——Nobody can contest a measurement made by a judge.

. . . competing exhibitors in the BOB/V competition wants to protest the height of the Winners dog?
A——This is permissible. Irrespective of previous wins, unless the dog has already been measured by the judge, a protest can be lodged against any dog in the ring prior to marking of the book.

. . . a competing exhibitor wishes to protest an entire class, can he file a blanket protest?
A——No, protests must be made individually directly to the judge on each dog, one at a time, designating the animals by armband numbers.

. . . you wish to refuse to honor a verbal protest?
A——You cannot refuse a verbal protest as long as it is made prior to the marking of the book and is made by a competing exhibitor in the ring at that time.

. . . as you placed the dogs beside their respective winning numbers and are about to mark your book, an exhibitor comes up to you and says he wants to protest the height, weight or color on dog number so and so?
A——You must accept and act on his protest.

. . . a written protest is filed on the winning dog?
A——This is not the judge's concern. Written protests are reviewed by members of the show committee, or their designees, and such reviews are not made during judging.

. . . you suspect a protest may be lodged against a particular dog on weight or height, should you go ahead and weigh or measure the animal?
A——No. Only do so if in your own mind you question the dog's physical characteristics and eligibility requirements.

. . . someone tries to file a written protest on lameness after judging of that breed is completed?

A——This is not the concern of the judge but written protest on lameness after breed completion cannot be entertained. Lameness is left entirely up to the discretion of the judge of that breed, day and ring.

   . . . you make an error in your judge's book?

A——Correct all errors with proper notations and your initials.

   . . . you noticed the error after turning your book in to the superintendent/show secretary?

A——If you discover the error before leaving the grounds, go to the office and make the necessary corrections on the original and all copies.

   . . . you are on your way home from a show and find an error as you mark your catalog from the pink sheets?

A——There is nothing you can do at that point. On the first working day, call the Show Records department of the AKC and advise them of the error and its correction. Confirm this phone call with a letter.

   . . . you are judging the group and a dog appears with the wrong armband?

A——Have your steward recheck the catalog with the exhibitor of the dog to be sure he has the proper number. Then, if necessary, contact the superintendent/show secretary who will check the breed sheets.

   . . . you are judging BIS and a group winner appears that is the wrong breed from what you have in your book as having won that particular group?

A——Get the superintendent/show secretary to review the group judge's book. If it appears that the judge may have inadvertently marked the wrong breed as winning, he may still be on the grounds and can make the necessary correction immediately.

   . . . that judge is no longer at the show?

A——The superintendent/show secretary and field rep will have to talk with the owner or exhibitor of the dog in question, determine the corrections that have to be made and make the necessary changes in the book. This is not a matter that the BIS judge becomes involved in and he should stay out of all discussions.

. . . you forget to pick up your catalog and pink sheets?

A——Write to the superintendent/show secretary and ask him to mail them to you.

. . . you are judging the companion show the next day?

A——Don't pick up your catalog or sheets until you have completed all companion shows. If there are different superintendents, they will mail your items to you.

. . . you are missing some pink sheets?

A——Sometimes your copy of the judging sheets get mixed in with some other judge's. Usually if this happens that judge will forward them on to you.

. . . you only judge a few breeds and would like to keep your hand in by handling someone else's dogs without charge?

A——Judges, even those who have approval for only one breed, are discouraged from handling a dog owned by another party. They also should not co-own animals solely for the purpose of showing them.

. . . you only judge a few breeds and want to continue showing your own dogs?

A——There is nothing in either rules or AKC policies that prohibits judges from owning, breeding and/or showing their own dogs. An extremely controversial subject in all elements of the fancy, abuse— either real or imaginary—comes from fellow judges trading wins or future assignments.

Suggested Reading

Booklets available without charge for a single copy from the American Kennel Club, 51 Madison Avenue, New York, NY 10010:

Rules Applying to Registration And Dog Shows

Guidelines for Dog Show Judges

All booklets sponsored by breed clubs representing those breeds you are either interested in judging or already judge.

Individual breed books written by recognized authorities covering your breeds.

The following general purpose, judging and moving books:

THE ART AND SCIENCE OF JUDGING DOGS, Brown, B & E Publications

THE COMPLETE DOG BOOK, American Kennel Club, Howell Book House

DAIRY CATTLE JUDGING AND SKELETON, Yapp, John Wiley & Sons

THE DOG IN ACTION, Lyon, Howell Book House

DOG STANDARDS ILLUSTRATED, Howell Book House

DOGSTEPS—ILLUSTRATED GAIT AT A GLANCE, Howell Book House

THE INTERNATIONAL ENCYCLOPEDIA OF DOGS, Dangerfield and Howell, Howell Book House

JUDGING DOGS, Smythe, John Gifford, Ltd.

LEO C. WILSON ON DOGS, Hasberg and McCarthy, Robert Hale & Co.

NICHOLAS GUIDE TO DOG JUDGING, Nicholas, Howell Book
  House
POPULAR DOG SHOW MAXIMS, McCandlish, Popular Dogs Publishing Co.
SHOWING AND JUDGING DOGS, Halmar, Arco Publishing
TAKE THEM AROUND, PLEASE, Horner, David & Charles, Inc.
THE WORLD ENCYCLOPEDIA OF DOGS, Jones and Hamilton,
  Galahad Books

Judges hold a revered position in the dog fancy.
Cummin—GAZETTE, American Kennel Club